Awakening to God

The Sunday Readings in Our Lives

YEAR A

Fran Salone-Pelletier

Awakening to God

The Sunday Readings in Our Lives

TWENTY-THIRD PUBLICATIONS

185 WILLOW STREET • PO BOX 180 • MYSTIC, CT 06355
TEL: 1-800-321-0411 • FAX: 1-800-572-0788
Bayard E-MAIL: ttpubs@aol.com • www.twentythirdpublications.com

The Scripture passages contained herein are from the *New Revised Standard Version of the Bible*, copyright © 1989, by the Division of Christian Education of the National Council of Churches in the U.S.A. All rights reserved.

Twenty-Third Publications
A Division of Bayard
185 Willow Street
P.O. Box 180
Mystic, CT 06355
(860) 536-2611 or (800) 321-0411
www.twentythirdpublications.com

ISBN:1-58595-349-0
Library of Congress Catalog Card Number: 2004106803
Printed in the U.S.A.

Dedication

To my family and friends
who have been the bread of life for me.

To my college professor Margaret Mooney
whose question, "Why don't you write?"
was seed firmly planted in my subconscious
for late harvest.

Special gratitude goes to my husband Jean,
my constant companion,
challenging and consoling me
as I look into the darkened mirror and see Light.

Acknowledgments

I am extremely appreciative of the warmth and cooperation that Bayard/Twenty-Third Publications has extended to me, and I am especially grateful to Gwen Costello, who saw possibilities to awaken a wider audience to God's presence. I am also in awe of the superb and meticulous editing done by Mary Carol Kendzia, who always managed to safeguard the timbre and tone of the reflections' content while honing my words into sharpened quality.

Contents

Introduction

These reflections on the Sunday readings were born from my own deep-seated, personal need. Along with so many other Roman Catholics, the Second Vatican Council awakened me to the Scriptures. I noticed that the Bible was no longer being treated solely as an academic subject or a text used to prove a point. There was a deeper and fuller meaning to be gleaned from the biblical commentaries I read in preparation for teaching Scripture.

I soon discovered there were more questions than answers. How did the readings apply to my own daily life? What did they really mean to me? How did they affect me in my decisions and my choices, in my struggle in developing a relationship with the God of my belief, and in my relations with others?

The more I pondered, the deeper I probed. I began to notice how much the Scriptures were helping me. To my great surprise and delight, they also assisted those with whom I worked in ministry, community Bible groups, and the person in the pew.

The uniqueness of these writings lies in their flexibility. They can be used in Scripture study groups by utilizing the questions to facilitate discussion; as prayer starters for individual or communal retreat experiences; as homiletic tools; as spiritual reading, with or without the reflective questions; to assist those who participate as catechumens or sponsors in the Rite of Christian Initiation of Adults, as well as those in liturgy-based catechetical programs; to prepare for a more prayerful experience of Sunday liturgy, and more.

What I have written is the result of my own prayerful reflection on the Word, as I hear the Lord speaking to me through my life experience. Though personal, this word—as well as the suggested prayer at the end of each reflection—is also universal and meant for the People of God.

Awakening to God is a series of wake-up calls, challenges to plumb the depths of God's word. It commands a keen attentiveness to the God who is present to us always, if only we will allow ourselves to be alert to the divinity in our daily lives.

Deeply grateful for all that God has given me,
I now give what I have received as gift to God's people.

1

Season of Advent

First Sunday of Advent

Isaiah 2:1–5; Romans 13:11–14; Matthew 24:37–44

Advent is pregnant with life, laboring with expectancy

Each time the Advent season rolls around, I have the impassioned desire to hear a pregnant woman reflect upon the readings. The power of love embodied in pregnancy would certainly emblazon the least fervent among us with fiery expectancy. A woman with a swollen belly is both a practical and a profound image of the vitality that we carry within us—a life that stretches us without breaking us. Theories that explore life in its continuum present us with truth, to be sure, but the practical, personal experience of bearing life from its earliest moments hums with conflicting emotions.

Exhilaration is tinged with anxiety. Eagerness is framed with concern. Beaming bliss is marked with waves of nausea. As is said of death and dying, so can it be true of birthing: physically, psychologically, and spiritually, life is changed—not ended. Ultimately, preparing for life is hard work that yields great rewards.

I remember well the excitement with which my husband and I greeted the news of our first venture into parenthood. We thought that nothing could replace the intensity of that feeling. That is, until it happened again and then once more. Each experience was unique and each was indefinably identical. Preparing took on different meaning with the coming of each child. Changing a room into a nursery was nothing compared to helping a child learn to be a brother or sister! Despite all the differences, being pregnant with new life was a common bond for everyone in our family.

As I look back on the experience, I see that it had, and continues to have, far-reaching implications. What was a common bond in our family is also a commonality we share with all of the human family. We are, all of us, pregnant with new life. Together, hopefully, we will all labor to give birth to that life and sustain its existence.

Advent is the gestation period in our Church year. It is the time we give ourselves to wait and be readied to receive renewed vitality. It is our new year, our new season, our new cycle of awareness. As is true of all generative moments, transformation is occurring. At first, the metamorphosis is invisible, unnoticeable. Slowly, it alters both parent and child. Once the sole occupant of a solitary body, now two dwell in one flesh. Mother glows with unusual vigor. Growing infant within pushes outward, announcing its presence to the world. I see in this bulging hillock of flesh more than a physical sign. I see burgeoning incarnation that cannot and will not be contained. I see life that refuses imprisonment, however comfortable the cell, however wondrous the womb.

As it is in the physical world, so it is with Advent. This is our preparation time. This is the period when infant Christian and parent Church alike are nurtured. Slowly, quietly, but with some degree of pulsing activity, they grow. Together, they are being prepared for the fantastic phenomenon of incarnation. What was once an idea, a carefully treasured promise, is becoming real—and really creative. Birth is in the offing. Nonetheless, it cannot be understood or cherished unless time, energy, and knowledge have been devoted to the process. Labor always precedes life. When all is well the labor is one of love and the resultant life is replete with loving.

And thus we are reminded, "You know what time it is, how it is now the moment for you to wake from sleep" (Rom 13:11). We cannot be passive during this transformation. If never before, now is the time for us to wake up, be alert, take notice. Once begun, there is no stopping the advent of life. There is no way, save death, to arrest the conversion.

During these four weeks before Christmas, we gather as the people of God to prepare and be prepared for birth and re-birth, both individually and communally. Ours is the work of climbing the Lord's mountain, not the hills of our human desires. We look for opportunities to be instructed in the ways of peace and nonviolence. Infant seeking to be born and parent pushing to give birth—both are new creations. Both give evidence of life's radical quickening.

Swords of injustice mortally pierce the very heart of humanity. Lest they demolish us entirely, we must beat them into plowshares of equality. Instead of training for a battle that kills and divides us, dissecting our unity into divisiveness where the powerful wage war against the powerless, we are called to effect peace-filled parity. Rather than walking in the darkness that causes us to stumble and fall, we are to walk steadfastly upright. Affirmation must replace negation, proposing instead of opposing, looking deeply into hearts rather than gazing superficially at appearances. Living honorably is our preference. We are called to waken from the sleepwalking existence we once labeled life, called to dance in the Sonlight.

Advent is not a season of quietude, though it is a time for silence and contemplation. We pause to reflect upon the the "night far gone," as well as "the day that is near" (Rom 13:12). No room is given to despairing over what has not been said or done, nor are we to be consumed with guilt because of our sinful deeds. There is simply the recognition that the darkening night has had its influence, but it is not the finality.

Day is drawing near.

In its fullness, Advent is a seductive force, a siren song of promise. Plodding forward, we remember our past, bear our present, and walk into our future despite deterrents. With Advent awareness, we are being drawn to the dawning of that day. Impelled by its promise, intrigued by its unexpected arrival, we wait patiently. We wait hopefully. Alert, aware, and anticipating, we seize the day as if it were our last—and prepare as if we had a thousand more. Ours is a pregnant life laboring with expectancy.

Advent people know that birthing is happening in our midst. Surely, we don't want to miss it!

For Reflection and Discussion

- How can you carve out time and space for quiet contemplation during this Advent season? Name some "swords of injustice" you have wielded against others. In what ways have you experienced injustice perpetrated against you? Against your faith community? How can the institutional church turn its own swords into plowshares? In what ways do you see yourself as an infant laboring to be born? As a parent pushing to give birth?

Prayer

God of our birthing, Spirit of our laboring, we come to you as infants yet in the womb of creation. We ask your help in making incarnate the wonder and compassionate care you show for us. Let the day draw near and the darkness of our night disappear as we wait in hope and joy for your coming into our lives, now and forevermore. Amen.

SECOND SUNDAY OF ADVENT

ISAIAH 11:1–10; ROMANS 15:4–9; MATTHEW 3:1–12

Bound in the Spirit

Sometimes it seems as if the Scriptures paint a picture of impossibilities— impossibly unreachable, impossibly untouchable, impossibly impractical. To think about a time and place where opposites live together harmoniously and communally appears to be a waste of time and energy. I can hear my husband's usual retort, given when I present him with ideas that suggest unorthodox combinations of people or concepts. "It'll never happen!" says he. "You're wasting your time!" says he.

Neither daunted nor deterred by his skepticism, I follow the path I have been given. Probably this dogged determination, this indomitable spirit, has been my trait, a gift, from birth. Knowing my parentage, it may even be a genetic predisposition! Surely, my college days proved to be a most intense feeding ground for this spirit.

I remember clearly the trepidation and tingling delight I felt when first I stepped foot on the campus of the College of New Rochelle, then a Catholic women's school on the outskirts of New York City. I experienced an amazing combination of emotions. I was concerned, anxious, worried, exhilarated, eager—all at once and with the same intensity. My grammar and high school days were over. Youth, in a sense, had died. But, intuitively, I knew there was, in this place, a shoot sprouting, a bud blossoming. The rarefied air of a college environment would also be a birthing spot.

During our first days on campus we were introduced to a Spirit song. Actually, it was far more than an introduction. Everywhere we went, the strains of its melody could be heard. It seemed as if the trees whispered the refrain across branches and leaves. The syncopation was permeating the marrow of our young bones. It was meant to be a mantra of creativity…the music of challenge.

If you ask us what's the spirit, well, it's mighty hard to say…
Hard to put your finger on it, but you know it's here to stay.
There's nothing spooky 'bout our spirit, it's as real as it can be.
It invades the halls, bounces off the walls, from the Castle to the "T."

Oh, it tiptoes through the Chapel,
And it whistles through the elms…
If you listen, you can hear it…
That's the Spirit, that's it, that's the Spirit!

CNR, as we would forever know her, was a holy mountain where there would be no harm or ruin but only knowledge of God filling the earth as water covers the sea. It was there that we were to learn what it meant to be inspirited women, roots of Jesse, signals for the nation, beacons of light, life, love, and truth. From our first footsteps, the clarion call was heard: reform your lives, re-form them, the reign of God is here. Change was paramount. Not modification for its own sake, it was transformation—for our sake, and God's.

The song we heard was not simply a cheer leading us to scholastic victory. It was a symbol. It signaled new life, new creation. We could not hear it and perceive its fulfillment in words alone. Hearing meant believing in possibility. Believing impelled acting as if it were true. Acting led to accomplishing, realizing what we now felt pulsing in our deepest being.

The message was clear. We were women of Spirit—Spirit-led, Spirit-fed, Spirit-bred!

Far from priding ourselves with the claim, we knew that ours was a call offered to many and accepted by few. Ours would be a life as collegiates who would never be allowed to rest on couches of mediocrity, nor pause for long to relish laurel crowns of glory.

We would be baptized in waters of wisdom for the sake of being formed and re-formed throughout our lives. These four years were to be entry points into an ongoing education. Life would always be a learning process—leading us out of our various darknesses into the light of truth and justice. This birthing place would serve as a nursery, preparing us, winnowing, threshing, making our response to service all the more perfect.

We would not be chaff to be burned in unquenchable fires. We would be unquenchably fiery women of Spirit.

I do not recall any overt message in this regard. It was a subtle infusion, a subliminal instruction. God's universal reign was ours to empower. Questions surrounding it were to be answered individually—and posed communally. Is harmony possible among flawed humans? Can ever we speak as one voice, praising and glorifying God with all the names divinity claims? Can we accept each other as we are as well as challenge each other to image God for God's glory?

Our present, indeed our presence, would hold promise and invite hope. It is now and will continue to be an offer that promises hope—hope rendered in judgments made with justice and decisions accorded rightly. Wherever we go, ruthless ones will be stricken by the power of our words; the wicked slain with the breath of our spiritedness.

Our advent into the world of commerce, education, medicine, art, social work, marriage, religious life was to be a "debut of difference." Women of Spirit, we would be different and make a difference. Where we are, there can be no poor people crying out in vain, no afflicted ones left helpless. Where we go, God's name is to be blessed and divine happiness experienced.

Women of Spirit, we make our choice "advent-urously." With each passing day, we renew and recommit our dedication. We choose to seek the glorious dwelling that defines reality.

So can you!

For Reflection and Discussion

- How can you initiate and nurture harmony in a flawed community? What specific means can be used to promote acceptance of each other as we are as well as challenge each other to image God? How is life a learning process for you and for those whose path crosses yours?

Prayer

Spirit of the living God, fall afresh on me.
Spirit of the living God, fall afresh on me.
Melt me, mold me, fill me, use me.
Spirit of the living God, fall afresh on me.

Spirit of the living God, move among us all.
Make us one in heart and mind, make us one in love.
Humble, caring, selfless, sharing.
Spirit of the living God, fill our lives with love.

Journeying through the flowering desert

"Be patient, therefore, beloved, until the coming of the Lord" (Jam 5:7). How easily those words fall from our lips when we use them as advice for someone else! How much they pinch and prick when we hear them spoken to us!

Strangely, the older I get, the more impatient I become. I am restless with bones that will not bend immediately and effortlessly upon command. I am perturbed when I must repeat, more than once, for those whose hearing is more impaired than mine. I am annoyed when my welcome silence is pierced by conversation's noise. I am frustrated when the thirty pounds that insidiously appeared to amplify my flesh will not miraculously and instantaneously disappear. Optic floaters invade to disturb my field of vision, names elude recall, time refuses to stand still. Pills stacked in neat piles have replaced the carefree "cuppa coffee and away I go." Schedules supplant spontaneity. Garage doors slam shut before the sun has set, bringing the day to an early end when once it had just begun.

I want my old self back—my young, lithe, sharp-sensed, quick-minded *me*. When Advent calls for newness, aging is great reason to be angrily impatient! The desert I traverse is a wasteland devoid of youth's dewy freshness.

Yet, deep within the well of my spirit there is a renewing spring of hope. In time's prison, the urgency of freedom becomes more acute. Slowly, reality hits. All those catalysts to impatience are also gateways to life lived truly and deeply if I steady my heart to the tempo of God's nearness *now*. Rather than falling into a retrospective view that is a stumbling block to transformation, I look into the power of the present moment—and see possibilities.

No pill is greater than God's immanence, no potion more awesome than divine transcendence. The wonder is that we are privy to both. God is as close and vital as our own heartbeat and as far beyond our reach as the most distant star in any unknown galaxy. There is no other to whom we can go, nor is there anyone else for us to seek.

Each of us finds God "out of the ordinary." In out-of-the-ordinary places, people, times, events that comprise our personal and communal history, we find God. Extraordinary divinity is disclosed in the commonplace if we do not clutter our sight by "waiting for another" (Mt 11:3).

Before our eyes life's desert begins to bloom. No longer is it a place of arid desolation with nothing but stinging, shifting sand and hot, dry winds to plague our steps. Feeble hands receive and accept strength. Weak knees are made firm with purpose. Frightened hearts are given strength enough to arrest terror and accept trust. Blinded eyes open, deafened ears are made clear. "Then the lame shall leap like a deer, and the tongue of the speechless sing for joy" (Is 35:6). Life blooms where death had held court, and we rejoice with joyful song.

To journey through the flowering desert is to meet with joy and gladness and flee from sorrow and mourning.

All it takes is patience—waiting with an indomitable spirit of endurance, "suffering" with passionately, death-defying persistence—as God comes into our lives.

This is good news, and we are the poor ones to whom this news is preached. The dryness of our existence is moistened with the waters of spirituality. We are awash with baptismal promises made in the wastelands we call home. In all the prisons in which we keep ourselves bound, the works of Christ are heard. Somehow, some way, God's will penetrates the rigidity, reaches the marrow, and continues to be done.

No longer are we reeds swaying in the wind. Nor are we clothed in the luxurious garments of pomposity. Those postures of aridity and apathy—the ambiance of indecisiveness rather than the advent of divinity—are removed forever. Only with deliberate defiance can we bring them back

We are the people of God. We are prophets foretelling God's word in a world that prefers to have its fortune told in optimistic palm reading or through a crystal clarity that removes all need for faith that walks with sight unseen. We are kings in a consumer society devoid of regal grace, graciousness, and giving. We are priests offering mediation and safe passage into the providential realm of goodness. We are messengers, sent ahead, to prepare the Way as we journey.

There is in us, least born of the kingdom, a sanctity that surpasses all understanding. Ransomed and renewed, we return to the God who has never left us, the God who sets captives free, who loves the just and protects strangers, who thwarts the way of the wicked. Returning, we discover anew that we are to be good news for all who cross our path.

The discovery flowers our desert lives causing us to bloom with the patient suffering that accompanies birthing. Seeing and being seen, there can only be reports of healing, freedom, and removal of stumbling blocks. We are God's blossoms in an arid land, God's promise of fidelity in an era of superficiality. Where we are sorrow and mourning will flee. Joy and gladness will prevail. The parched land will exult and all will see the glory, the splendor, of our God.

For Reflection and Discussion

- Describe times in which you have felt a desert dryness in your spiritual life or in the life of your faith community. How did those times—that parched land—lead you into the splendor of God? When and where have you met God in the ordinariness and the out-of-the-ordinariness of your life—in the places, people, times, and events that comprise your personal and communal history? How can you steady your heart to the tempo of God's nearness now?

Prayer

God of my Advent days, I hear your message to go forth and be good news to a downtrodden world. Yet I am afraid. I am unsure of myself and feel inadequate to the task. I beg you to strengthen my feeble hands and make firm my weak knees. Give me the words to say that will give ease and encouragement to those whose hearts are frightened, as well as the wisdom to be silent when necessary. Instill in me a passion for freeing all who are oppressed. Most of all, help me to be the person you have called me to be. Amen.

FOURTH SUNDAY OF ADVENT

ISAIAH 7:10-14; ROMANS 1:1-7; MATTHEW 1:18-24

Birthing the God within

Whenever I read the Matthean infancy narrative I feel the anguish of two good people who were flying in the face of the law and customs of their people. Here was an unwed mother trying to tell her fiancé that she is pregnant—but not with his child—and is, as well, still a virgin. Three facts, one more astoundingly incredible than the other, were his to swallow.

He faced equally difficult decisions. Would he commit her to the legal punishment she deserved and he was allowed? Would he accept the inevitable sneers and jeers of his contemporaries in order to save her reputation? Perhaps it would be easier to avoid both options and quietly divorce her. In any case, his ego was damaged and confidence in her was shattered. All their hopes and dreams of an ordinary marriage and family were wisps in the wind of fate. Life had been cruelly twisted into a mask of death.

Or had it?

The saving grace for this couple was their willingness to ask for a sign from their God. In their confusion and dismay, they did not hesitate to request some divine indication of the path they were to take. Fear of wearying God would not stand in the way of faith in the tirelessness of providence. There were no holds barred. The sign could be "deep as Sheol or high as heaven" (Is 7:11).

Too often we fear to ask for signs of God's presence in seemingly impossible situations. Fear grips us, imprisoning and blocking our freedom to be believers. Rather than daring to reach for the stars, we settle for the mundane within our reach—and close our eyes to the possibilities lying within the impossible. Faith seeks to see signs of divine presence and rejoices at the clear vision. Fear denies their presence and mourns the inadequacy of life.

Both Mary and Joseph asked for clarity—and received conviction.

This did not make life any easier, just simpler. Joseph simply believed what he was told by Mary and by the angel. His belief gave him strength. It empowered him to deviate from his original plans and give God a chance. It allowed him to take a deep breath and go forward with the planned marriage despite the reality that this union would be unique and confusing to many. Wedded bliss would carry pain in its joy, agony in its ecstasy. Mediocrity would not mar their existence. Justice would replace legality; surprise would take the place of superficiality.

Mary was equally troubled. Her questions erupted from the depth of her soul. Messianic music hummed in her veins, perhaps more fluidly and rhythmically than it did in other young women of her day. The stories, the promises were her earliest memory. They were told and retold as only a nation of persecuted exiles could relate them—with the fervor of fidelity in a God who would save them. Knowledge was not enough, however. Mary needed to expand her understanding. "How can this be since I do not know man?" she asked.

Wonder, amazement, worry; the emotions tumbled through her being. She had asked her question and was given the courage to accept the answer. Both Mary and Joseph chose to follow the direction of God's spirit, no matter how incredible it might appear to be. Resolute in their conviction, they believed that incarnation is the sign which is deep as the nether world and high as the sky—and were willing to birth the God within them.

Their choice...their decision to say "Yes!" awakened them to salvation. Similarly our choices will do the same for us.

Boldly, we need to remove the shackles of Ahaz from our lives. We need to ask our questions, all our questions, without fear of wearying God nor terror of being wearied by the requests. God has promised to be our Emmanuel, God within us, individually and communally. We can scarcely discover that tireless, divine presence without maintaining an awareness that questions reality. What is it all about? What is God's will for us? In what ways are we to respond to it? Are we living in such a way that we are fulfilling God's prophecy for us?

Questions abound. Signs will be given. Direction is available. Advent's season of watching and waiting is swiftly coming to a close. Now is the time for us to birth Emmanuel—and be birthed into humanity's promised salvation. We are in the throes of a labored expectancy that will impel divinity into our midst. If we tighten the muscles of terror now, we will create unnecessary pain instead of riding the crest of the Spirit's power. Inspiration's breath will be the saving reward for our toiling tremors. God is with us; God is with *us*!

The reality of the nearness of God-made-flesh pierces every corner of creation. God who does not live in time or space has given divinity to both. Nothing, no one, has ever been the same. Our humanity, flawed as it is, has been changed and made holy. God has entered our lives as no one else has, before or since, nor will in the future.

We need to make room in our worldly womb for the presence of the God within. We need to name the Babe of Bethlehem, calling him Jesus because he will save his people from their sins. We need to recognize the name of our savior.

Have no fear of the child within.
Christ will be birthed from within uterine deeps.
Blessings will be received.
All will ascend the mountain of divinity,
stand in the holy place, and see the face of God.

For Reflection and Discussion

- Where are you in this saga of signs and faith? In whom, when, and where do you see God? How and when have you asked to see signs of God's presence? How and when have you responded by being those signs for others? In what ways are you afraid to see and believe, to believe and see?

Prayer

Emmanuel, God-with-us, open my eyes to the gift of your abiding presence in me and in others. Help me to make room in our worldly womb for you. Let me be a birthing force of lively faith in the face of all who seek to enforce fear and death. In these last "laboring" days of expectancy, allow me to be ask for signs of incarnation that are as deep as the nether world and high as the sky. Amen.

Season of Christmas

ISAIAH 9:1–6; TITUS 2:11–14; LUKE 2:1–14

Walking in darkness, seeing a great light

Usually my protestation about this time of year is "I am not a Christmas person," but Midnight Mass at Christmas holds a special spot in my heart. I retain reminiscences of New England Yules with their bitingly cold dryness and sparkling bright stars that twinkled with delight in inky black skies. As I dressed in holiday finery, bundling up to leave the cozy warmth of my house to enter that frozen night, I recall experiencing anew life's strange juxtapositions. Brightness married to gloom; warmth wedded to chill; night holding hands with day—all packaged and beribboned, ready to be given and received.

Now the night grows dark and heavy with expectation. People wait and remember. Anticipation increases with each passing moment as midnight approaches. It seems as if everything has stopped for a moment. Breathless eagerness is palpable.

In many cases, the world *does* stop. Traditionally, cease-fire commands are given in countries where war is in progress. Non-Christian peoples show respect for the beliefs of Christians and reverence remembrance of the coming of Jesus. All the world gathers its deepest feelings and awaits birth.

Churches everywhere glow with an incandescence no candle or light fixture could possibly render. It is noted—not always graciously—that church congregations grow at Christmas. Folks who rarely join the assembly are drawn to church with an inexorable impulsion. Differences are made delightful on the day when "a child has been born for us, a son given to us; authority rests upon his shoulders; and he is named Wonderful Counselor, Mighty God, Everlasting Father, Prince of Peace" (Is 9:6).

Unity born in diversity is the gift of Christmas presence.

It was—and is—a holy night bursting with graces to thaw my frigid soul. On this night, uniquely, I can come to terms with all that speaks of war, argument, oppression, slavery, imprisonment. The land of gloom now shines with a great light that will not allow the darkness to dominate. You and I have walked in darkness. We have voyaged in that abyss long enough to recognize truth. In our darknesses, we have seen a great light. It has shone on us. Now—and forevermore—we are people of the Light.

No burdens can yoke us to despair. Nor will our taskmasters retain their rod-like power over us, smashing us into submission. We sing a new song—and a weary world rejoices. The days of our confinement are completed. Birth is happening in our midst. Love reaches its apex, crying out in unison with the infant entering a world we have created. Life and love are wed and we are born of the union. With nothing to fear, we proclaim good news, tidings of great joy to be shared by the whole people. This day a savior has been born: the Messiah!

Everyone is touched by the birth of the savior. All feel the upsurge of hope, the removal of fear, the smashing of yokes that have held us down. We see the pole of worry and isolation breaking into splinters. This day, this holy night, is a time to celebrate the release of all that has kept us bound. It is a feast of universality. All are freed; no one has anything to fear. God is gifting humanity with divinity, with brotherhood and sisterhood. God is stooping to conquer, bending down to place us into a kingdom of peace and justice. God's favor rests on us. We are heirs to a reign of godliness

As it happened in Bethlehem more than 2000 years ago, it occurs this night. Birth comes while we are confined to ordinariness, doing what we must do, being who we are. Crowded out of comfortableness, birth happens in out-of-the-way places where no one else will go.

There is no special spot, time, or sacrifice demanded for divine entry, only an accepting spirit. We are touched in the "busyness" of our everyday living, going about the daily tasks and duties of our vocation, as were the "shepherds living in the fields, keeping watch over their flock by night" (Lk 2:8). We are touched by One who hurts with the poor, oppressed, weary, burdened outcasts of society. We are touched by a message that promises to remove the terrors of night, replacing them with the good news of daylight. We hear hope in the midst of hopelessness and find peace in the fragmentation of war.

We are especially touched by the marvel that the One and the event are not constrained by time and place. They are not restricted to the warmth of past memories. The birth of the Lord Jesus is yesterday, today, and tomorrow—a tomorrow that is forever.

Believers and unbelievers alike are struck by both the One and the event. Somehow we want and need this birth to happen in the darkness of our individual nights. We want and need it to be a midnight experience. It must happen at a time when deep quiet pervades our dark night. Walking in the hush of blackness, we are more able to feel the piercing power of God's great light.

This day our God has chosen to become one of us. Touching God and being touched by God is our good news! It is the reason we live fearlessly. Touched, saved, made holy by our God Immanuel, we are empowered to share with everyone the evangelistic message of possibility in the face of impossibility. Christ, the Child of Promise, pierces dire reality with the radiance of dreams. Mangers, not palaces, become the significant havens of birth. Poverty, not riches, brings power. Service, not manipulation, is our strength. Blessed with the gracious humility of a God who loved us so much that he became as small as a baby, we live in paradox and grow into godliness.

Wonder-Counselors, God-Heroes, Princes and Princesses of Peace, our rule over the earth is to be gently forgiving, mercifully just, and justly merciful. Potent with the zeal of the Lord, our cry of praise explodes into the atmosphere permeating it with joy. "Glory to God in the highest heaven, and on earth peace among "those on whom God's favor rests" (Lk 2:14).

We walk in darkness to see a great light.

For Reflection and Discussion

- When have you heard the message in your heart that Christ is born to you today? What were the circumstances and how did you respond? How can you participate in empowering justice and peace in your own world? In your own life situations?

Prayer

O God, with Whom is the well of life, and in Whose light we see light; increase in us, we beseech Thee, the brightness of Divine knowledge, whereby we may be able to reach Thy plenteous fountain; impart to our thirsting souls the draught of life, and restore to our darkened minds the light from heaven. Amen.

— Mozarabic Sacramentary (before 700 AD)

Family dreaming

My daughter's words ring in my ears. "Why does it always have to be me who does the changing and makes the compromises and ignores the hurts?" Her question strikes deep into the mess and mire and miracle we call family.

It is not easy to be a family. It is more difficult and desirous to be a holy family. Forming, nurturing, and sustaining relationships is a lifelong challenge. Doing so within a family framework commands and demands continuing effort. "Why me?" is now translated into "Why not me?" The question pierces through personal preferences and bares for view individual opinions. Subconscious or unconscious jostling for position rears its ugly head. Old hurts and new needs vie for attention. Family intimacy can be as formidable as it is forceful.

Everyone appreciates the idyllic portrayal of loving brothers and sisters reared by perfect parents. All know, as well, that reality proves to be quite different. Choice is understood competitively rather than as selection for service according to ability and giftedness. Heartfelt mercy, kindness, humility, meekness, and patience are virtues to be accepted appreciatively as honored gifts. They are not so easily shared with relatives who appear to be less willing to give than they are to receive. Perhaps the greatest burden comes with our lack of choice in the matter. The old adage, "You can pick your friends, but not your relatives," bears a truth that is hard to dismiss.

How do we love those with whom we are stuck for a lifetime, people who are connected to us by birth but not by election, individuals whose identity too often provides a mirror image we insist is distorted?

As problematic as this may be in our families of origin, it is intensified as we wend our way through and with the family of God—the people connected to us by baptismal birth, not by election!

To honor a person's authority when we have not had a vote or voice in the choice is difficult. My daughter's question reverberates in the challenge. To dedicate oneself to thankfulness and find lasting root in the kindness and consideration shown to "church fathers"—even when their minds fail them and their weaknesses have taken hold—is almost beyond believability. Yet, this is the way we continue to be and become family—God's family.

Still the question remains: how do we achieve such holiness without losing individual integrity? How do we maintain the sanctity of true self in the face of submission? How do we change "why me?" into "why *not* me?"

I suggest that an answer, perhaps the answer, lies in family dreaming.

Joseph faced the impossibility of his life via dreams. As he was told—and did—so must we. Family dreaming allows each of us to get up from our doldrums, our anxieties, our concerns. It allows us to get up and take the child we have buried within our "adult" selves and flee to our Egypt, run to the place of prayerful solitude God has prepared uniquely for us. Flee, not for permanent escape but to avoid having our innocent integrity destroyed. Flee solely for temporary safety, staying only until God tells us otherwise. Remain until God calls us out of that Egypt, calls us to be family.

Personal prayerfulness feeds family dreaming.

As we pray, our dreams persist and intensify. All that seemed incredibly impossible becomes manageable. Dreams thrust us into the reality we feared to enter. They come in the brilliance of day as well as the darkness of night. Dreams arrive when we sense a lack of faith—and during those times when our faith is most intensely felt. Dreams are God's way of breathing divinity into all we had considered to be merely human. Inspired, we are able to continue being and doing all that God is asking of us—even when it appears to be nonsense, even when it involves incomprehensible hardships. Daily, we can set out for our "land of Israel"—the perfect family, the wondrous family of God. It matters not what route we take. Our primary concern is to safeguard the child within each of us, and to thwart those who have designs on the life of that child.

Each of us, by turn, is father and mother for the infant divinity we carry in our human spirit. Each of us is called to safeguard that spirit by letting the word of God, rich as it is, dwell in us. This is our starting point. Being prayers allows God's word to make its home in us and take hold of us. Its richness will nourish our poverty. Its vision will empower our dreams. Personal qualms and quirks will not disappear. They will appear and be seen differently. Uniqueness will become manifest gift. Giftedness will demonstrate itself in wisdom made perfect. Wisdom will empower us to "teach and admonish one another in all wisdom; and with gratitude in your hearts sing psalms, hymns, and spiritual songs to God....in the name of the Lord Jesus" (Col 3:16–17).

And we will be heard—as a family dreaming!

A family dreaming can never be a family scheming. It cannot succumb to the vagaries of power, position, or prestige. There will be no family secrets to keep us apart nor structures of deceit to manipulate and cause bitterness. Authority will be founded and grounded in an authenticity that begs imitation and transformation. Each member's dream will be honored as God-given, divinely inspired to intensify family holiness and individual sanctity.

The worth and value of each person will be sought, uncovered, rediscovered, and held in high esteem. No longer will the question, "Why me?" plague and disturb us. It will not hound "our child" into hiding nor search to destroy it. In its stead there is family dreaming. Always there is the child's life to protect and new lands to enter. Blessedness is ours as we walk in the way of God—together in a unity that defies separation and defines differences.

Becoming a family means taking a chance on God—and following the truth discovered uniquely in dreams.

Never will family dreaming end. Please, God!

For Reflection and Discussion

- In what ways can you assist your faith family to begin or to continue dreaming? How can you implement this style of living in your biological family? What examples can you give from your own life experience that affirm the statement: "Dreams are God's way of breathing divinity into all that we had considered to be merely human?"

Prayer

God our Creator Parent, our Redeeming Nurturer, and Sustaining Spirit, breathe into us your ever-renewing presence. Let the holiness of your family union with its Triune diversity ever inspire us to dream dreams and see visions. Fill us with the courage to flee to the Egypts you have chosen for us. Urge each of us to protect, enjoy, and become the child you have parented, an image of your divinity. Empower us to recognize and thwart those who would destroy that child within so that we might grow in wisdom, age, and grace before you and all humanity. Amen.

THE SOLEMNITY OF MARY, MOTHER OF GOD

NUMBERS 6:22–27; GALATIANS 4:4–7; LUKE 2:16–21

Treasuring all things with heartfelt reflection

One of the most profound honors we can give to the woman who gave birth and nurture to Jesus of Nazareth—and thus became our mother, as well—is to ponder the powerful phrases that describe her. In all the hubbub of that Bethlehem birth, Mary was an oasis of peace. Shepherds "went in haste" to find the family of three. No mention is made of what those shepherds were thinking or expecting. Only their desire for discovery is noted. Whatever they had in mind, what they saw was a catalyst to understanding all that they had been told concerning this child. Seeing was enlightenment. It was also empowerment. To see was to be able to speak of the vision and share the insight.

Whenever I have gained understanding, I have raced to find someone to tell, to describe and explain as well as exclaim the news. Would the shepherds not have done the same? I can only imagine the excitement and chatter in that place. And "and all who heard it were amazed at what the shepherds told them the shepherds" (Lk. 2:18).

Yet Mary, who might well have been the one most astonished and amazed, remained serene. Instead of reacting to the feverish pitch surrounding her, she responded to it. Two simple but intense actions were hers: "Mary treasured all these words and pondered them in her heart" (Lk 2:19).

Treasuring and reflecting: there is the core of Mary's solemnity, the heart of her maternity and the essence of her sanctity. Mary could have considered herself to be a treasure. She could have reflected upon her own importance, felt its power, and accepted the shepherds' visitation as her due. But she did not. She chose to view them as a precious presence, pondering their giftedness as God's graciousness. The woman we celebrate today was a woman who treasured all things and gave them heartfelt reflection. She was a woman who let God's face shine upon her, look upon her kindly, bless her and give her peace.

Mary allowed God to be God, believing that God would inspire Mary to be Mary.

It is altogether possible that she did not completely understand the implications and complications of this birth. That was of no concern to her. For

Mary, it was sufficient to treasure all these things. It was enough for her to see the preciousness of birth, life, visitors—even in the strangeness of a manger located in a place so far from her home. Mary expected nothing. All was gift—even her child's name!

Gifts were never received or accepted with superficiality. Mary did not offer scarce glances at beribboned presents or spare glimpses at bedraggled persons. She looked deeply into everything and everyone, recording what she saw and sensed for remembering and reflection. Being—simply to be— was given supreme importance. It was blessed with divinity.

The solemnity of Mary is ours to imitate as well as celebrate. We are called to the same degree and intensity of life—where all is treasured and reflected in our hearts. We are asked to accept simplicity, experience serenity and reflect upon all that God allows to happen. Hold everyone and everything as heartfelt presence. Understand God's presence. Let God's face shine upon us, bless us, and keep us. Permit God to look upon us kindly and give us peace.

Let God be God and believe
That God will inspire us to be who we really are.

Because Mary let God be God she knew no chains. She lived as God intended us all to live. Mary chose God, freely, even blindly. When God called, she acquiesced, without fully understanding what was being demanded. She selected her answer without being forced but out of desire. Each stop along the way was chosen. Alone with an angel who spoke of terrifyingly pregnant possibilities, together with Joseph in a cold, uninviting stable, racing fearfully along the road to Egypt, tearfully treading Jerusalem streets, paining with the sight of Calvary's cross, mourning within Jesus' tomb, bravely present to anguished disciples in an upper room—Mary had choices. She could have said "No, not this time." She could have opted out of the pain. She could have submitted to numbing denial or given way to terror, doubt, hopelessness, or despair. But, she did not. Mary always chose God's way—and trusted.

Her individuality is made credible precisely through her choices. She is not an either/or person but one who embraces both/and. Mary lives the reality of being both maid and Queen; virgin and mother; daughter and bride. She supports us in our quiet presence as well as our active leadership. Mary understands what it means to be emptied out—and to be filled. She knows the pain of watching her beloved one suffer and the power of basking in hearing him be praised. Mary is witness to the slavery that fear brings and to the compassion that empowers that same fear with faith. Mary's beauty is her humanity, a solemnity she lived day by day, if not moment by moment.

I recall a saying that was bandied about, years ago, often written on banners and posters: "Today is the first day of the rest of your life." Mary asks us to modify those words. Her solemn request is that we remind ourselves that "Today may be the last day of our life."

Give this day your heartfelt reflection. Seize it with love and treasure it accordingly!

For Reflection and Discussion

- What examples can you give that testify to the reality that you are a person who treasures all things and reflects upon them in your heart? Who are others in your life that do the same for you? What do you think and feel about the statement: "We are close to God only to the degree that we are free?" Are there chains that bind you from trusting choices? How can you free yourself from them?

Prayer

My soul magnifies the Lord, and my spirit rejoices in God my savior, for he has looked with favor on the lowliness of his servant. Surely, from now on all generations will call me blessed; for the Mighty One has done great things for me, and holy is his name. His mercy is for those who fear him from generation to generation. He has shown strength with his arm; he has scattered the proud in the thoughts of their hearts. He has brought down the powerful from their thrones, and lifted up the lowly; he has filled the hungry with good things, and sent the rich away empty. He has helped his servant Israel, in remembrance of his mercy, according to the promise he made to our ancestors, to Abraham and to his descendants forever. (Luke 1:46–55)

FEAST OF THE EPIPHANY

ISAIAH 60:1–6; EPHESIANS 3:2–3, 5–6; MATTHEW 2:1–12

Following a star to find another route home

I have never been particularly interested in scouting or camping out, but star gazing has always fascinated me. Memories of eighth-grade astronomy classes, with their mandatory nocturnal neck-craning to find the constellations, race across my mind as I now lift my wrinkled senior citizen face skyward. The sparkle of a dark, wintry, bejeweled night still has me catching my breath with awe. I cannot say that I have ever followed a particular star. I have kept one in sight for long moments, however, imagining a voyage across time and space in darkness illumined by the brilliance of a solitary star.

Following one star demands faith. All other stars must pale, fading into unimportance, in the presence of a chosen luminary. Tiny sounds, lost in the clamor of daily noise, become signs of invisibly powerful presence. Creatures of the night are as intensely exciting as they are intriguingly elusive. As I sense their availability without actually seeing them, I receive a renewed understanding of God's omnipresence.

To follow a starlit path is to find that there are other routes to take and additional companions to assist us as we journey home. On the way, epiphanies happen. We discover that we, too, are magi traveling life's path with one goal in mind, one search in focus. We seek to find a messiah king. It is too much for us to discover a crucified savior or a risen Lord. Both experiences push the envelope of credibility and stretch the horizons of faith. Instead, our quest ends—and begins—with a newborn Babe. Our journey is one that enters the labyrinthian paths of interdependency.

The first stop en route is a logical one. We make our way to the persons in positions we believe would keep them informed and most able to direct us. "Where is the child who has been born king of the Jews? For we observed his star at its rising, and have come to pay him homage" (Mt 2:2). Both question and statement disturb the powers-that-be. Babe or not, homage is to be paid to them alone in order to maintain the status quo. Any hint of change attacks and challenges basic claims of bedrock stability.

Modern day Herods surround us. Desiring control and fearing the cry and call of divinity, they pretend interest while planning to inject fear and frustrate God's plan. Subtly and overtly, they tell us to "Go and search diligently for the child; and when you have found him, bring me word so that I may also go and pay him homage" (Mt 2:8). Mouthing reverence, their real intent is removal.

Herods of all stripes in all places and times are persons with murderous desires. God's existence is so terrifyingly real, so totally consuming, so incredibly freeing that it must be eliminated. Their survival depends on divinity's demise. With escalating terror of losing royal kingship, they demand the destruction of all whose claims are viewed as challenge to their throne. Wisdom is sacrificed on the altar of information. Superficiality is given honor and homage. Power and prestige overwhelm giftedness and supplant treasured talents with mediocrity.

We magi, magical in our determination and eagerness to unearth God's presence wherever it may be found, find life and joy in the search. We are members of God's family and sharers of God's promise. God's glory shines upon us. Nations shall walk by our light. Raising our eyes to look about, we see that all gather and come to us, from near and far. Our participation in the epiphany event is expansive. It empowers and includes others.

Unlike Herodic influences, our impact on humanity is authentic. Its authority rests in truth; its power is manifest in serene justice. We seek not to frustrate God's plans or to murder innocence, but always to be encouragers. Majestic in our efforts to bear and bring giftedness to light, we enter God's house...our hearts....and find the Babe of Bethlehem awaiting our arrival.

As we offer homage to God, newborn in our lives—prostrating ourselves before divinity—we come face to face with real epiphany expectations. Golden with the glow of grace, we shall also encounter bitter suffering—the myrrh that perfumes existence with the aroma of profundity. Coffers of carefully guarded plans, predilections, and possibilities are laid before the God who loves us. All that we are and wish to be is presented as gift, returned to the Giver.

This tiny Babe, God Incarnate and savior of all, lies before us with an expectancy that is larger than life. His dependency mirrors our own; his mission unfolds as will ours. His message becomes ours. Internalized daily, it is as comforting as it is challenging. Always, it provides a pathway into peace.

Despite pressure and persecution, shunning and silencing, cloaked in normalcy, the Babe of Bethlehem will follow his own star, journeying home to the God who gave him to us. He will grow to be the Carpenter of Nazareth, Prophet of Jerusalem, Resurrected Savior of both Gentile and Jew.

So will we be "epiphanized" into costly greatness. Our route home will have its price. We will need to evade and elude those who would happily herald us into deadliness. Instead, we find and follow our own star, heed and honor our own dreams. Following the starlight of those dreams, we will go home by another route—and lead others along the Way, to Paradise!

For Reflection and Discussion

- In what specific ways can you lighten and brighten the path for other pilgrims to find their way home to Paradise? How do you understand the fact that the route home will have its price? Jesus of Nazareth had to follow his own star on his journey home to God. Describe the "star" you feel you must follow at this age and stage of your life. Who are the Herods who deter your pilgrimage? Who are the magi whose gifts inspire you?

Prayer

We three kings of Orients are; bearing gifts we traverse afar.
Field and fountain, moor and mountain; following yonder star.

Refrain: O Star of wonder, star of night, star with royal beauty bright,
Westward leading, still proceeding, guide us to thy perfect Light.

Born a King on Bethlehem's plain, gold I bring to crown him again,
King forever, ceasing never, over us all to reign. (Refrain)

Frankincense to offer have I; incense owns a Deity nigh;
Prayer and praising gladly raising, worship him, God on high. (Refrain)

Myrrh is mine: its bitter perfume breathes a life of gathering gloom:
Sorrowing, sighing, bleeding, dying, sealed in the stone-cold tomb.
(Refrain)

Glorious now behold him arise, King and God and Sacrifice;
Alleluia, alleluia! Sounds thru' the earth and skies. (Refrain)

— John H. Hopkins Jr. 1820-1891

THE BAPTISM OF THE LORD

ISAIAH 42:1–4, 6–7; ACTS 10:34–38; MATTHEW 3:13–17

What do you want to be?

Every time I read the section of Isaiah presented for our prayerful reflection on this feast day, I remember my father. Daddy was a stern man, an immigrant Italian father born in the Victorian era and twenty years older than my mother. He brooked no breach of his authority. Neither did he make allowances for imperfection. I can remember being taught, as a tiny tot, to speak "the proper Italian" in lieu of the dialects both he and my mother spoke. If the job was to be done, it would be done well or not at all. That was the way he lived his life. That would be the way we would live ours!

Daddy could show his love for us only in devoted labors and continuing demands. It was a serious love that stretched our abilities, but never to the breaking point. His rare forays into frivolity were usually spontaneous bursts of song—most often operatic arias. Simply stated, he was a hard taskmaster. He was also a genius who loved challenge and discovery as well as the heated air of a debate—at least until we grew old enough to produce facts that bested him at his own game! Then we were summarily dismissed with his favorite conversation ender: "You talk like a sausage! Comin'a down to earth."

But, that is not the memory evoked by the Isaian passage. Instead, I recall a wonderful moment when my father must have been contemplating my future. Though the circumstances and details have faded, I can still clearly hear him asking me one "simple" question: "What do you want to be?"

Though probably neither he nor I was aware of it at the time, the question never probed the possibilities of doing or achieving as society might ask. It was always about being and becoming, about growing, challenging, changing.

The question reverberates with each path and passage life's choices bring. It is a question that encourages hope, provides possibilities, and widens horizons. It is a question properly posed by a prophet. My father was my Isaiah. Though he remained tongue-tied when it came to pronouncing me his chosen one with whom he was well pleased, he was certainly quite articulate in his belief that he had put his spirit on me. And so he has!

At his best in my memories, my father images my God. He upheld me through all my dreams, providing me with the education by which I could fulfill them. He also managed always to provide a place for himself somewhere in those potentialities! If he was to be by my side, I was to be by his. I was being baptized into his family with its unique call and commitment, its possibilities and promise.

My Dad believed in me. He believed that I could be anyone I chose to be and do anything I chose to do. His plans for me were open-ended, flexible enough to include any number of changes. He asked only that I always improve in the process! When I sought and attained a graduate degree in theology, he beamed—not at the choice of subject since he was not particularly a promoter of institutions, but at the growth indicated by the new diploma. When I left my teaching post in the public school system to work for the church, he was equally happy because he viewed my title, Parish Director of Religious Education, as a promotion from the classroom. It was the dynamism of life that my Dad appreciated, respected, and encouraged. What he was unable to accomplish in his own life, my father handed over to me to do in his name.

I read Isaiah today and my Dad's presence is enlivened. So is God's. I see my God looking at me with love. I hear my God identify me as a chosen one. I begin to realize how much God has invested in me. God hands over to me the responsibility of discipleship and the privilege of carrying on the work that defines that role. God counts on me to be his envoy—no more or less than God counts on you! We are people who are called for the victory of justice. We are those whom God grasps by the hand, forms, and sets as a covenant of the people, a light for the nations.

Our task is clear. We are "to open the eyes that are blind, to bring out the prisoners from the dungeon, from the prison those who sit in darkness" (Is 42:7). What is not so clear is the how-to. Again, my father's sage advice springs to mind. Whenever I complained that I did not know how to do something or I did not understand, he would respond with his dual methodology: "Just dope it out! And use your 'genuity." After all, it worked for him.

Dope it out! Use your 'genuity! Watch and listen, look and learn, try, fail, and try again. In the process, the correct answer will come. With those continued efforts, we begin to see the truth of God. Our own blindness lessens until we have the clear sight necessary for leading others along the path of righteousness. We begin to recognize the many ties that have bound us to trivialities and details. Freed from those restraints, we are able to bring out those who have spent their lives in prisons of fear and doubt. We are empowered to release those confined by unnecessary limitations.

Unafraid, we travel together. We leave our dark dungeons of cynicism, negativism, and disbelief to walk in the light of the Lord. No longer are we stuck in terror of making a mistake. Instead, we freely, bravely, lovingly dope it out—with God in our midst to affirm us as we use our 'genuity.

We take a chance on the potency of God's belief in us, just as I still recall the power of my Dad's belief in me. As we walk into the wonder of each day, miracles happen. It is as if the words of Peter are sounded with each footstep taken. Everywhere we are, everywhere we go, they can be heard. We need only to insert our individual names to make the message come alive for us today. "You know the message he sent…how God anointed (insert your name) with the Holy Spirit and with power; how (insert your name) went about doing good and healing all who were oppressed by the devil, for God was with him/her" (Acts 10:36, 38).

What was written about Jesus can be said about us. We, too, are the beloved sons and daughters of God on whom God's favor rests.

So, let's use our God-given 'genuity and dope it out!

For Reflection and Discussion

- How have you allowed God to submerge you into the waters of your baptism? In what ways do you see yourself as an anointed and beloved son or daughter of God? How are you doing good and healing all who are in the grip of their various devils? Who are the bruised reeds in your life that need your assistance lest they break?

Prayer

God be in my head and in my understanding;
God be in my eyes and in my looking;
God be in my mouth and in my speaking;
God be in my heart and in my thinking;
God be at my end and at my departing. Amen.

—Sarum Primer Prayer (1514)

The Baptism of the Lord in the life of Kathleen Henderson Heath

I can yet remember my return home from the funeral of a valiant woman who lived freely and faithfully as a member of God's family. My heart still throbs with the plaintive cry of Taps and the mournful tolling of the last call for Shallotte Rescue 2373. The silent comradeship of fire engines and rescue vehicles that led the way to the cemetery carried me into a profound speechlessness. I understand that her pain is now over, that Kathleen is home where there is no more weeping, no more chemotherapy or bone marrow transplants, no baldness to proclaim the devastation wrought upon her already frail body. Yet, I hurt with loss. I suffer with the lived reality of baptism—a baptism into suffering and death as well as rebirth into resurrection.

Kathleen died exactly as she lived, simply a servant upheld by God, chosen to bring forth justice to the nations, not crying out, not shouting, not making her voice heard in the street. She was a bruised reed that did not break with or from her blemishes. She was a smoldering wick that would not allow cancerous growths to quench her flame. She was a postal worker who took her work seriously, though always with a smile. No purchase of stamps was too small, or task too great. Forgotten zip codes were eagerly traced. No problem dismayed her.

Entrusted with mail that carried heartfelt wishes, business papers, congratulatory notes, jokes to cheer or sorrows to bear, Kathleen knew somehow that those missives were the means by which God used her to open the eyes of the blind, to bring out prisoners from their confinement. She recognized that her baptism was effected in the daily tasks of the postal service. It did not matter that she did not understand it completely, only that she lived it consistently.

Her "day job" was not enough for Kathleen. Baptism was to be a complete submersion or it was nothing at all. So she expanded her horizons to enlighten the sick, to be their house of light. Interestingly, her choice was to join the Shallotte Rescue Squad. I wonder if she ever thought about that fact. Baptism, for all of us, means that we are to be members of God's rescue squad. Kathleen took that quite literally! When most everyone in the church pictorial directory was photographed dressed in their Sunday best, she and her husband chose to wear their everyday best: the uniform of the rescue squad.

From tech sergeant in the Air National Guard to plumber, member of the Shallotte Point Volunteer Fire Auxiliary to wife, mother, and grandmother, daughter and sister, catechist and friend, Kathleen showed no partiality. Rather, in every person she met she saw someone who feared God and acted uprightly. Acceptable to God, each was acceptable to her.

From the given description, one would think that Kathleen had garnered honors from every quarter of life. One might expect to find plaques prominently displayed and kudos beyond expression. That was not the case. Her labors were done quietly and without fanfare. They were significant only to the recipients, and even then were not given recognition.

Kathleen imitated John the Baptizer. I could hear her saying, "I need to be baptized by you, and yet you are coming to me?" Jesus came to her every day— to be baptized. Of course, it was not the Jesus of Nazareth who arrived. It was Emmanuel, the God who lives with us, the Christ who is in us. Christ came to Kathleen in those who waited in her line at the post office, those who received her aid from the ambulance, those who talked with her in hospital corridors and waiting rooms. Christ came to her in her family members and friends, neighbors and acquaintances. And Kathleen greeted him in each and all.

At a Christmas party she attended less than a month before her death, Christ tenderly gave her hugs and received them in return. Her fragile body could scarce contain the illumination that came from within its depths. No halo would shine as brightly as her eyes did that night. Kathleen was a member of God's family and she would miss no celebration they had planned. I remember glancing in her direction as she sat a few seats from me. I saw a woman who lived for others. Instead of commenting upon her obviously failing health to gain sympathy and attention, she noted only she was up and about. It was good news she wanted to share. And so, she went about doing good for all of us who were present—healing us of our oppression. Laughter took too much energy. Smiling replaced it, smiling and brightly intense gazes that sear hearts with remembrances. It was as if she were taking everything into her being and, in some mysterious way, storing it for our use. Certainly, it was for my benefit. I am empowered to write words that pour tearfully from my heart, words that are living waters flowing generously— renewing, refreshing, and recreating.

After being baptized in those waters, immersed and submerged in their healing powers, I am able to see Kathleen anew. She is no longer a "was" but an "is." All that happened in her life, I begin to view as fitting for her and for us. I cannot pretend to understand her baptism of fire that had no flames, but I do believe it was meant for her righteousness and ours. More importantly, I believe that Kathleen allowed it to happen. I am convinced that she lived her faith fearlessly, even when she was afraid. She leapt into the darkness time and time again, in the trust that God leapt with her, holding her lest she be harmed.

This last baptism, like her first, would be a baptism into death. This time, the resurrection would be final and complete. This time, she would come up from the water and behold the heavens opened up for her. She will see the Spirit of God descending like a dove and coming upon her. And a voice from the heavens will speak, saying, "This is my beloved daughter in whom I am well pleased."

The baptism of Kathleen Henderson Heath is finalized. Ours is still in progress. The ending to our life story is already written. We have but to live it to completion, believing that we are grasped by God's hand, formed and set as a covenant of the people, a light for the nations. Baptized into death, we will rise again in glory to see God as God is—and to see each other as we really are.

On that day each of us, with Kathleen, will smile and say, echoing the words of God the Father, "These are my beloved brothers and sisters, with whom I am well pleased" (Mt 3:17).

For Reflection and Discussion

How have you allowed God to submerge you into the waters of your baptism? In what ways do you see yourself as an anointed and beloved son or daughter of God? How are you doing good and healing all who are in the grip of their various devils? Who are the bruised reeds in your life that need your assistance lest they break?

Prayer

God be in my head and in my understanding;
God be in my eyes and in my looking;
God be in my mouth and in my speaking;
God be in my heart and in my thinking;
God be at my end and at my departing. Amen.

—Sarum Primer Prayer, 1514

Season of
Lent

First Sunday of Lent

Genesis 2:7–9, 3:1–7; Romans 5:12–19; Matthew 4:1–11

Blind sight

From the time I was a little girl I have resented the fact that life's ills have been laid at the feet of a woman who was enticed by forbidden fruit. No one ever mentioned or questioned her apparent power or intelligence. There was never any comment regarding the fact that she chose what was presented to her as an unreasonably denied good. She was duped by cunning—a primordial serpentine con artist.

Two trees were said to be growing in the middle of the garden. God's command that the one in the middle be avoided now becomes rather confusing. Which one in the middle bore the forbidden fruit—the tree of life or the tree of the knowledge of good and bad? But, the woman and her husband already had the breath of life blown into them. They were already inspired and infused with divinity. There must have been a moment of real bewilderment.

In the midst of it all, somehow, the woman recognized a connection between the trees. Did she believe that life is both effected and affected when one knows the difference between good and evil? Perhaps it was an intuition that good and evil are intermixed in life. Did curiosity pique her interest? Certainly death was not considered to be part of the equation. She would not have chosen that option.

Whatever impelled the woman, she picked and ate a variegated fruit that was pleasing to the eyes and desirable for gaining wisdom. Unselfishly, she shared it with her husband. There is no hint that she wished to ease her guilt by implicating someone else—only that he was there with her. Sharing was her natural instinct.

Having eaten, they realized that the wisdom held captive in the fruit of Eden's tree gave both of them sight. It was, however, a blind sight that revealed their nakedness and caused them shame. No longer were they able to see themselves—their naked, vulnerable selves—as good. Gone was the unabashed delight they had in each other—just as they were, with no pretense or expectation. Abasement replaced innocent acceptance. Disgrace entered where grace had abounded.

Their eyes were opened to their true selves—and they were blinded by the sight!

That momentous experience began the continuing human battle against blindness. Generation after generation we have been encouraged and challenged, coaxed and coerced to fight for sight. It is not so much a return to original innocence that we are seeking as it is a renewed vision of vulnerability. It is a trek into transparency where our very soul, our inspirited being, is revealed—both to ourselves and to those whose paths we cross. The fig leaves of fiction we have sown together to mask our goodness and clothe it with prideful pretense slowly disintegrate in the heat of the humility. We may continue a lifelong journey seeing as if in a mirror, darkly, but sight will be ours.

The process is one best recognized when we give ourselves the time and treasure of desert experiences. Lent is a marvelous opportunity for us to open our eyes—without being blinded by what we see. These forty days of "deserted" pilgrimage, an annually renewing event, can bring us face to face with our graceful, grace-filled, gracious selves—if we enter the land of Lent led by God's spirit, not our self-centeredness.

It is here, in this place of arid beauty, that we will fast in order to discover our true hunger. Here we meet the tempter who seeks to seduce us into settling for food that meets immediate needs but leaves us aching to fill the void found in an empty heart. Here we will face our irresponsibility. Placing all the blame and work on God, our refusal to respond to the divine invitation to be and become real people will be clearly apparent.

In Lent we learn that blind sight is worse than no sight at all!

Where Adam and Eve seemed to have had a pleasant, pleasurable time in the garden, Jesus' desert period was spent in fasting and prayer. There was no grand choice of fruit from a variety of trees. Jesus' boundaries were quite different from those of the first humans. His was the limitation accepted when divinity took on humanity. Jesus knew and embraced the fact that he would no longer solely eat from the fruit of the tree of total divinity without somehow encompassing his humanity. Fasting for forty days and nights, he showed us the radical commitment he had made to take flesh and dwell among us. His hunger was real, as was the vulnerability of body and spirit that overtakes anyone who has endured such a physical denial. Yet, he would not succumb to the temptation to eat what was now out of bounds for him. For Jesus, there was no cover-up. There was only continuing revelation. His nakedness did not bring shame; it granted glory. He would not mask his vulnerability with false divinity but would unveil it in true humanity. Jesus saw clearly—and adoringly gave homage to the God in whom he lived and breathed and found his being.

Prayer made all the difference. Speaking and listening to the Father, sensing the call and power of the Spirit, Jesus contemplated his own, personal, reality. Any questions he might have entertained were subjected to the clear light of prayer and profound silence.

His was not blind sight

With open eyes he knew the dangerous path he would trod in the pursuit of justice and the propagation of mercy, but he did not hide from its peril. He did not clothe the naked facts, except with prayer that strengthened and enlightened.

Lent affords us the opportunity to choose to select once again a pilgrim's path. Lent creates a space and place for soul-searching. It returns us to memories of lush gardens of innocence and arid deserts with mountainous choices. Lent is life seen under a microscope as well as a magnifying glass. It brings us into direct contact with the clay of our earthiness and the breath of divinity blown into our nostrils so that we might live.

Lent opens our eyes to all that we are, giving sight to our blindness and gracing our blind sight.

For Reflection and Discussion

• Do you believe that life is both effected and affected when one knows the difference between good and evil? How is that true—or untrue—for you? Blind sight revealed human nakedness, caused shame, and denied worth. How do you see yourself? Are you blinded by the sight of your true self or enlightened by it? In what ways might this lenten season help you to gain real sight?

Prayer

God of the desert come to me in my dryness and moisten my spirit with love.
God of blindness assist me in my sightlessness with light from above.
God of creation instill in my mortality a spark of divinity's life.
God of boundaries retrain my boundlessness and lead me from strife.
God of suffering teach me the passion that brings joy quite absurd.
God of all knowledge show me the wonder of living your word. Amen.

SECOND SUNDAY OF LENT

GENESIS 12:1–4; 2 TIMOTHY 1:8–10; MATTHEW 17:1–9

Arising to fearlessness

I live in a Southern retirement area where golf courses are as enticingly prevalent as the gray-white heads and arthritic limbs they lured into residence. The sunshine, blue skies, and laid-back lifestyle are hypnotic. Everyone and everything moves at a slighter slower pace. Volunteerism replaces paid employment—motivated both by good intentions and the convenience of choosing the time, place, and frequency of one's work. Never before was this possible. We are in control—and the feeling is great! Without a doubt, our common cry is "Lord, how good it is for us to be here!"— quickly followed by a universal plea for friends to come join us on this mountaintop of exhilarating enjoyment.

It is easy to resonate with Peter's sentiments on the Mount of Transfiguration. We all prefer to pitch tents and remain where elation resides. We want to capture peak moments and freeze-dry them for future hydration when life becomes dry and desiccated and dull. Cameras flash, camcorders whirl—for the same purpose. Hold that pose. Maintain the experience for instant replay and longterm remembering.

There is nothing wrong with the human desire to remain where life is pleasant. After all, "Jesus took with him Peter and James and his brother John and led them up a high mountain, by themselves" (Mt 17:1). It was not their initiative but that of the Lord that brought those three men to their heady heights. Jesus must have agreed that it was good for them to be there. On that spot, far from daily toil and trouble, he chose to let them really see him. But they missed the point of the vision!

They thought they understood what was happening. Without further examination or reflection, they believed simply in what they saw and felt at the moment. It was good enough for them. In fact, Peter, controlling the situation, was still speaking—overriding any possible implications of the reality— when the truth overshadowed him. "This is my Son, the Beloved; with him I am well pleased; listen to him" (Mt 17:5).

What we see is *not* what we get. There is more! Listening to the Lord is required before we are able to discover and uncover the depth of our vision.

What do we hear when we stop to listen to the Lord? We hear just six short words that could change our lives, if we let them. Six words bearing two commands would and could make all the difference: "Get up! Do not be afraid!"

That's it! Get up! Arise from the deadly doldrums that kill us with malaise and apathy. Quit lying down, buried in blankets of reluctance, resistance, and refusal. Above all, do not be afraid! Place complete trust in the God who loves us more than we love ourselves.

The power of God's Good News comes when we hear it, fear it, and continue to be of good cheer in it! Cast away all fear of being discomfited or discouraged. Stop looking downcast and dreary over dire possibilities. Instead, look up and see the Lord— only the Lord and no one else. Look up to the Lord; listen to the voice of God. Let the sight and sound of divinity be our empowerment and energy. Discover the truth. Learn again a lenten message— to see sharply is not to remain in a stupor.

To see the Lord, dazzling and radiantly present, and stay in static contemplation was not enough for the apostles. It cannot be enough for us. We are meant to listen and live adventurously. Ours is a journey that leads us down from mountaintop experiences into valleys where visions become realities.

Sometimes the trail is clearly marked. The obstacles are visible and avoidable. Companions are compatible and numerous. Confidently, we march along at a good clip. However, at other moments, there will be a fearsome voyage into the unknown—the blind path of newness calling for our unique and personal trailblazing. Like Abram, we will be asked to go forth from the land of our kinsfolk—the place of comfort, ease, and support. Go forth to a land known only to God, hidden from view, to be shown us when the time is right. It takes only one small step to begin the voyage. What was said at the time of the first lunar landing is true for pilgrim Christians: "One small step for each of us; one giant leap for all!"

The mixed feelings of fascination and fear may cause us to freeze on the edge of motion. Dreading danger while courting courage we seem unable to move from our spot—until the lenten refrain returns empowering us to bear our share of the the hardship which the gospel entails.

"Get up. Do not be afraid"

Hearing, listening, looking, and seeing only the Lord—perhaps even holding our breath—that first tentative step is taken into the unknown mystery of Lent and onward to passion and resurrection. Following hopefully where we are led, a discovery is made. We are a changed people, one and all. Something profound and paradoxical is happening to us, with us, through us. Arising from our fear is a deeply rooted faith in God's promise. We begin to see glimmers of its fulfillment, shades of its presence. Another step is taken; a deepening truth is given and received.

"I will make of you a great nation, and I will bless you, and make your name great, so that you will be a blessing…in you all the families of the earth shall be blessed" (Gen 12:2–3).

The promise is mind-boggling, fit for a mountaintop experience and found in the valleys of tremulous life. There is but one requirement for its fulfillment, one divine request. Permit the touch of God to resurrect us from our fear-filled prostrations and protestations.

"Just do this for me—in memory of me—Get up! Do not be afraid."

When we look again, we shall see no one else but Jesus alone.

For Reflection and Discussion

- What do you think comprises a mountaintop experience of God? Have you had such an experience? What happened? How did it affect you? How might leaving one's comfort zone also be a peak event?

Prayer

Dear God, there are so many things I fear in life. So much triggers my desire to stay put, to remain in my own comfortable spot—spiritually, physically, and psychologically. I want to climb mountains and go into deep valleys with you, but I am afraid of the pain that might be involved in leave-taking. I believe that you are with me, blessing me as I go. Yet I stay stuck in my fear that the bright cloud of your presence will cast a shadow over my life. Touch me with your love and help me to rise from those fears. This I ask in the name of your beloved Son, my brother and savior, Jesus the Christ. Amen.

THIRD SUNDAY OF LENT

EXODUS 17:3–7; ROMANS 5:1–2, 5–8; JOHN 4:5–42

Strike the rock and find refreshing grace

Prayer is inevitably a self-confrontation. Its challenge is epitomized in the question posed in Exodus 17:7: "Is the Lord among us or not?" We take the radical risk of leaping into life and yet thirst for the Egypt we left behind. Frightened, exhausted, tattered and torn by the risking, we wonder at the worth of it all. Isn't the "devil we knew" far better a companion that this God we cannot fathom at all?

Trying the faith route only leads to discovery of more hardships and sufferings. It is no easier a path than the enslavement we had so eagerly relinquished. Still, we thirst; still, we hunger. Our loneliness has neither diminished nor disappeared. If the truth be known, we feel the pain and suffering even more sharply because this is the way we have chosen! Gone is the luxury of blaming someone else. Anguished, we wail, "Is the Lord in our midst, or not?"

It is too facile a response to say that God is among us and we must believe it. No matter how religious an answer that may be, it seems not to appease our thirst or soothe our pain. Like the Lord Jesus, we have to pass through our own Samaria. We need to take the shortest, most efficacious route to our spiritual destination. We have to ask the burning question.

Graciously, Jesus leaves us totally free. Jesus allows us to begin with all the petty problems we use as obstacles to slow progress and hinder growth. It does not matter how many times or ways we say, "Impossible!" Jesus replies with promises beyond our imagining. Answering not in kind but in depth, Jesus reminds us, "Those who drink of the water that I will give them will never be thirsty. The water that I will give will become in them a spring of water gushing up to eternal life" (Jn 4:14).

Repeatedly, Jesus tells us, the Lord is in your midst. The answer is within you. Look—there I am at the core of your being! Strike that rock —and find healing waters within. Jesus will already be standing there, waiting. All things are possible when we work together with God.

Too often we believe only because it might mean an easier way to live. "Give me this water, so that I may never be thirsty or have to keep coming here to draw water" (Jn 4:15). Faithfulness is yet to be achieved. However, God chooses not to berate the selfishness, but gently draws us more deeply into divine presence. God's transforming gentleness wins us over.

In *The Woman at the Well*, Adrian van Kaam explains it beautifully.

Each lost human self may have its own story of five or more husbands. We may have been wedded to fame and glory, to the gang, the in-group, the community, to money and success, to popularity, pleasure and power, to some social cause. We may have tried out some or all of them to find ultimate happiness and meaning in life. We may not have realized what we were doing. But the Lord knows, the innermost recesses of the human heart. Suddenly, his grace may touch us, incite us to confront ourselves and our unholy liaisons. At the same time he deepens in us the faith, hope and love that may carry us through such a crisis of self-discovery.

Our life situation is the "well" where daily we meet the Lord. At this wellspring we receive the invitation to give up something precious. It is there that the challenge to unfold a graced Christian life is offered us. Van Kaam writes:

If, with the Samaritan woman, we say yes to this call, we emerge as a new self in Christ. We bury the old self fixated on one "husband" after another. We rise anew in Christ; he will reveal to us our graced possibilities for growth in him. Like the woman at the well we, too, may be shaken loose from everything we believed we could humanly count on.

At such times our life may seem almost catastrophic. The shake-up may be so strong that it becomes impossible for us to retreat comfortably to what used to be. The woman meeting Jesus had reached a point of no return. She could no longer experience the joy of going back in a relaxed and unperturbed way to her past life. Her self-image is changed irrevocably under the impact of the perception evoked by Jesus.

The Samaritan woman quenched her thirst for a real relationship by revealing her weakest self to the stranger who was interested only in reflecting her truth and revealing his own. She tried every trick she knew to deflect his care-filled concentration, only to discover that she would not be moved from his loving response. Nor would he refrain from continuing revelation. Nothing drew Christ away from her. Not even the surprised return of his disciples could do it. Ignoring the woman standing there, they urged him to take care of himself. Steadfast in his caring, Jesus remained where he was.

She was changed. In a sense, so was the Lord. He was touched by this woman who came to understand him while his own disciples were still wondering who he was and what he was all about. She came to the well and discovered that refreshment was always available within her own truth. Her truth made her one with the Lord of Truth.

Wells are everywhere. In every desert place, for every desert person, we are oases witnessing to the Lord's strength. Powerfully compassionate, our God tells us everything we ever did and loves us all the while. Transformed by such great love, it is good for us to cry out: "Why did you ever make us leave Egypt?" It is good to be pierced with the question, "Is the Lord in our midst or not?" Each inquiry strikes at our rock-solid stubbornness allowing grace to penetrate. Healing waters can now flow freely for God's people to drink.

Only then will we be able to see ourselves as we are. Only then will we see with our hearts. Only then will the words of faith be integrated into our lifestyle. Made whole and holy, we can say, "It is no longer because of what you said that we believe, for we have heard for ourselves, and we know that this is truly the Savior of the world" (Jn 4:42).

Having opened our eyes to see, our ears to hear, we now truly believe. We have struck our rock-hard stubbornness and found refreshing grace.

The Lord is in our midst!

For Reflection and Discussion

- To what have you been "wed" during your adult years? How have those unions affected and effected your faith life? In what ways has your life situation been a well where you have met the Lord and been given spiritual water to quench your thirst? How can you assist your faith community to ask the question, "Is the Lord in our midst, or not?"

Prayer

God of healing water, I beg you to meet me at the wellspring of my life. Help me to see that I am in need of spiritual refreshment. Help me to know that I cannot find that strength in things or in power, prestige, or position. Let me look with honesty at my life to see it as it is, not as I pretend it to be. Give me the humility I need in order to hear you ask of me, "Give me a drink." Hearing, let me then go into the world in which I live and proclaim the wonder of your saving presence in our lives. Amen.

FOURTH SUNDAY OF LENT

1 SAMUEL 16:1B, 6–7, 10–13A; EPHESIANS 5:8–14; JOHN 9:1–41

Blinding vision

Karen, our neighbor's daughter, is a lovely young woman, married with two daughters. Her interest and enthusiasm for life is inspiring. She delights in everything. Her adventurous spirit draws others out from their doldrums and lifts their spirits. Those characteristics alone would make her someone special. However, as a result of a childhood accident, Karen is also blind.

I remember clearly the day we first met. Karen was visiting her folks when she learned about my husband's avocation—painting. Her immediate response was to ask if she could view his work. Taken aback by the request and feeling a bit awkward, Jean invited her to come and see. What we experienced that day will never be forgotten. Karen "saw" with her fingers as they flew across the paintings. She "saw" with her ears, listening to Jean's descriptions, and heard the art he had produced. She "saw" with her heart, commenting on each before declaring which one was her favorite. The inability to see as most men and women do was not an obstacle for Karen. It was—and is—a gift.

We are all called to that blinding vision. Ours is the vocation and mission to judge, not from appearance of lofty stature, but as God judges—by looking into the heart. It begins at home. Each of us needs to look into our own heart, compassionately viewing what is there and accepting who we are as God accepts us. Only then are we empowered to "live as children of light—for the fruit of the light is found in all that is good and right and true" (Eph 5:8–9). Only then will we be correct in our judgment of what pleases the Lord.

When I read the story of the Jesus' curing the man born blind, I think of Karen. Unlike the afflicted one in the gospel, her blindness remains. But, like him, God's works show forth in her. Lacking physical vision, she is yet "one who has been sent" to her family, friends, neighbors, coworkers. Yes, even to my husband and me. She has been sent to enlighten us about seeing and not seeing. Undistracted by all that assaults the eye, she teaches us how to unclutter our viewing field and regain focus on what is truly important. Hers is a blinding vision!

Her question is "Where? Where is the beach? I want to feel the sun, sand, warmth, salty breezes, and the tickle of a scurrying ghost crab. I want to hear gulls laughing, crying, and fighting over scraps of food."

To ask "where" is to open adventure's door and discover grace.

It is interesting to me that, as soon as they realized healing had happened, the blind man's neighbors and friends asked, "Where? Where is he?" They wanted to know the whereabouts of the one who opened blind eyes. One would suspect that they, too, had blind spots—searing sightlessness—in need of being healed. Perhaps curiosity impelled the question, or a desire to see for themselves. What matters is that they believed what they saw and sought to find the healer.

By contrast, the Pharisees asked "how?" How did this happen? Their query emerged from quite different motivations. They were interested in entrapment, not enlightenment; in deterrents, not discoveries; in exclusion, rather than inclusion. Questioning how the cure was attained, they began to cast doubt both on the healer and the healed.

Fear enters. Flickering flames of faith are put to the test.

Too often we are less like the blind man—who never asked for the gift of sight, but graciously received and accepted it—and more like the Pharisees. Our questions divulge a penchant for judgment, disbelief, and dismissal of those who do not fit within the parameters of the law. In the attempt to find something "illegal" to use as a battering ram, insincere questions barrage the innocent. When those prove ineffective, disparaging statements become the starting point. "First of all, we know this man is a sinner," they said—and so do we.

Accusations have judgment as their point of origin! Seldom do we look to see who we are, what we have done or left undone. Usually, it is a finger pointed at another's sinfulness so that we can appear to be blameless, or at least less evil, by comparison. And how do we arrive at our conclusion? It is based solely on legality, keeping or breaking the law. No consideration is given to the possibility that fracturing the letter of the law might be necessary to allow the emergence of its spirit. No regard is given to the higher law of love. No space is provided for compassion, understanding, or forgiveness. Within those restrictive boundaries, the righteous ones can label Jesus a sinner—and expel from their midst all who see as Jesus sees. Choosing to stay steeped in fear, they strangle faith.

The blind man models for us a totally different perspective on life. His rebuttal to accusation is to admit his own inability to make any judgment. "I do not know whether he is a sinner" (Jn 9:25). Such evaluations are not within the realm of consideration. He remains blind to them! All that is important is his own "conversion." Once blind, he now sees. It is as simple as that. With his new, blinding vision, all is changed.

Belief brought him sight; sight intensifies his belief.

Jesus came into the world to clarify the difference between true blindness and true sight—"I came into this world for judgment so that those who do not see may see, and those who do see may become blind" (Jn 9:39). His task was to reveal truth, provide light, and offer freedom And, he did it by spitting on the ground of rules and regulations, making of them "healing mud!"

When we are busy being persons who hide from the truth, extinguish light, and take away freedom, we are among the sighted who are yet blind. If we were blind, ignorant through no fault of our own, there would be no sin in that. But, we say that we see, yet act blindly—so our sin remains.

We have been given sight. Light has entered our darkness. Brightness has pierced dull mediocrity. No longer may we cling to the edges of clarity and charity. We must live as children of light, producing every kind of goodness, justice, and truth. We must be correct in our judgment of what pleases the Lord. Blindly going where we are sent, letting the mud and saliva of ordinary living be healing forces, "our faith, hope, and charity turn hatred to love, conflict to peace, death to eternal life" (Opening Prayer B).

For Reflection and Discussion

- What instances in your life have led you to cling to the edges of clarity and charity? How have you fallen prey to dull mediocrity in your faith life? When has self-righteousness blinded you to your own prejudices, keeping you from truth and real freedom? How has God provided opportunities for you to become truly sighted, and how have you responded to those opportunities?

Prayer

God of my blindness, bring me sight;
Allow my darknesses to flood with light.
Teach me the way to know my sin;
Let it provide a path for you to come in.
Anoint my sightlessness with graced mud and clay
That I might have blinding vision each day. Amen.

FIFTH SUNDAY OF LENT

EZEKIEL 37:12–14; ROMANS 8:8–11; JOHN 11:1–45

Empty graves, rising spirits

Every time I read the story of Lazarus' death I am struck by the confusing emotions expressed by those who were present. This time the experience was compounded by the fact that I had just opened and read an e-mail sent by an acquaintance whose wife had courageously battled cancer—and lost the fight in death. I wished I could have been there, although that was an impossibility—and probably a selfish desire that would have thwarted the opportunity for closer friends to share time with the family.

Perhaps Jesus felt the same way. Perhaps he knew that it was more important to allow the folks in Bethany a chance to befriend Mary and Martha—to be a healing presence for them—than it was for him to rush to their side. Perhaps it is more essential to feel the absence of a loved one than to be comforted with the presence of a friend. In any event, there is a crucial necessity for us to move from avoidance and denial to acceptance before we can find healing. We need to experience the emptiness of our graves before we can let our spirits rise.

I do not know how or when this happens. What I sense are the conflicting, confusing emotions involved in the process.

In her book, *The Joy of Stress*, Loretta Laroche captured the essence of those emotions. Using humor to convey her message, Laroche asked that we really look at stress and see that it does not cause us to be dry bones barely existing until we finally die. It does not mean lying in an empty grave and labeling it life. Stress can positively put flesh on our bones, if we let it. "Yesterday is history, tomorrow is mystery, today is a gift. That's why we call it the present," says Laroche. Life is one big opportunity.

Isn't that what God offers us today—the opportunity to live? Ezekiel tells us that it happens when we enter into the process. It happens when we command, "O dry bones, hear the word of the Lord" (Ezek 37:4). Somebody has to speak God's invitation. Jesus spoke. The living word enfleshed dry bones in empty graves, and spirits began to rise. Then he gave that mission to us.

Beginning with ourselves, recognizing that we are dry bones, we are reminded to listen. Hear the word of Yahweh: "I am now going to make the breath enter you and you will live" (Ezek 37:14). The experience of breathing life into our being is a moment-by-moment reality. Each event, encounter, experience that comes our way is now another chance to see God working to bring us to life.

It is messy work, making flesh grow. The result is invaluable: a person who knows who God is. To know God is to believe in our gut that God is in charge. God sets us free, to leave our empty graves and let our spirits rise.

Every once in a while I truly experience that freedom. In those moments I am Martha and Mary of Bethany. I can simply tell God that something terrible is happening in my life—without asking for anything. I can say, "The one you love is sick." Sick of the frustrations of coping; sick of being weak and imperfect; sick of trying with no apparent success; sick of journeying; sick of deciding and choosing; sick of reflecting and pondering. I am sick.

At other times, I speak about someone both God and I love. Words, prayers, lie fallow in my heart. I cannot ask for I do not know what to request. So, I say simply, "The one we love is sick"—and I leave it to God to decide what to do. I do not do this easily, nor without dismay. I fear that my words are not enough. My trust in the God of life wavers in the face of impending death. The stench of mortality is overpowering. It sickens and stops me from approaching the tomb of terror, from seeing God's grandeur, from believing that empty graves give rise to glorious spirits. In my sickness, in the illness of the one I love, I am dying. But I am also coming to believe that God is God. Deep in my being, I know God will come in time to save me from myself—not a moment too soon nor too late. I know God will not leave me in my pain but will join me there.

God cries when I hurt because I am God's beloved friend. God does not want me to rest in an empty grave when I could be a rising spirit.

Whether I am buried in a tomb of confusion, grief, disillusionment, despair, or sinfulness, I am loved—and impelled into being by that love. God comes to me and commands, "Come out!" Stumblingly, hesitatingly perhaps, but hearing the voice of my Lord, I emerge from my death-cave. I am Lazarus. God is my help.

Not yet totally liberated, the winding cloth of my own mediocrity and indifference impedes my walk. So bound am I by death's entwining garments that I am unable to live. My face is wrapped with fragments of fear. Blinded, I cannot yet see my way to life.

I have left my empty grave but my spirit has not risen from it. Tied and sightless, I stand and wait.

God, my help, has the vision I lack—and asks others to see and do for me what I am still unable to accomplish by myself.

"Unbind her. Let her go free. Empty that grave. Take away the storm, the obstacle that impedes.

Help her spirit to rise!"

At any given moment, each of us is Lazarus—bound, gagged, unseeing, needing, wanting to be set free. Each of us is Martha or Mary— sorrowing for our brother or sister—speaking to God of our hurts, our pain, our disappointment, our desolation, and waiting for response. We are, as well, Thomas— fearing yet daring to go to death with a friend.

Frequently, we are responsible bystanders with an ever-deepening ability to respond to pain. Our purpose and mission in life is simple: to unbind those who are enslaved and set them free to live. We are they who empower dry bones, to hear the word of the Lord!

Most of all, we are Jesus—weeping with love, dying to give others life.

We are the ones who console and comfort, challenge and confront. We are the healing helpers who seek to empty graves and let God's spirit rise.

For Reflection and Discussion

- How can you empower others to take away the stones of disbelief from their spiritual graves? In what ways can you be someone who loosens bindings and sets people free? When have you allowed others to set you free from your lifelessness? Which of the biblical characters best describes you today: Martha? Mary? Lazarus? The mourning friends? Jesus? Thomas? The disciples? Why?

Prayer

Watch, dear Lord, with those who wake, or watch, or weep tonight and give your angels charge over those who sleep. Tend your sick ones, O Lord Christ, rest your weary ones, bless your dying ones, soothe your suffering ones, shield your joyous ones, and all for your love's sake. Amen.

– St. Augustine

Passion (Palm) Sunday

Isaiah 50:4–7; Philippians 2:6–11; Matthew 26:14–27:66

The paradox of palm-waving passion

Is it strange to note that our entry into the holiest season of the Church year is marked by palm-waving yet steeped in suffering? Is it difficult to understand triumphal access being painted in the somber blues and purples of continuing pain? If these are foreign concepts, then we are not people of depth. We are not people who have experienced, firsthand and frequently, the mystery of life. Nor are we people who have grasped the reality that the cross is a sign of contradiction. That sign we so readily place upon ourselves, "In the name of the Father, Son, and Spirit," proclaims that we, too, are signs of contradiction. We are passion people whose view of life is "cross-eyed," but clear!

Passion Sunday is well-named. It is not Painful Sunday, nor Hurting Sunday, nor Wounded Sunday. Those names indicate irritating but momentary problems. Passion is a way of living, the way of life chosen by resurrection people. It calls us to an ever deepening realization of life's profundity. It asks that we accept, embrace, and empower freedom—in ourselves and others. Passion Sunday helps us to recall the fact that we are a gifted people chosen for service. We are a holy people, a royal priesthood, seeking to grow ever more completely into the image and likeness of God. Passion Sunday recognizes our feelings, gives them heed, voices them, and then asks us to remember always that ecstasy is the other side of agony. Neither is experienced without tasting the other.

No refusal to believe in our giftedness will change the fact. The Lord God has afforded us everything we will ever need to live radically—and to challenge others to do the same. Our gifts are not "extras," luxuries, or niceties to be placed on a shelf and admired. They are essential components of vitality. Unused, they wither—and we die.

What might these gifts be? Isaiah lists them readily. "The Lord God has given me the tongue of a teacher, that I may know how to sustain the weary with a word" (Is 50:4). We possess a capacity to learn and understand the power of enthusiastic encouragement. This has little to do with brilliant speech or having the exact words to say for each occasion. What we say is not nearly so crucial as how we say it. Our attitude, which "must be Christ's," heartens the disheartened and provides courage where discouragement pervades. To rouse the weary is to recognize our own weakness and fatigue.

In ways known only to our creating God, we are continuously and constantly being replenished. "Morning by morning he wakens—wakens my ear to listen as those who are taught" (Is 50:4). Each dawning day brings with it a newness known only to those who live passionately. Both overtly and covertly, God acts to open our senses, our person, our whole being, to the wonder of divine presence. God removes the obstacles that block our hearing and prevent the recognition of God's power. Having cleared the way, God gives us the power of divinity—to heal and forgive, to be rich in love and mercy.

However, God cannot and will not force us to be receivers. God does not insist that we accept all that is freely offered.

The option remains uniquely, individually, our own. It must be. Our acceptance of giftedness must be passion-filled, replete with suffering, copious with contradiction as was Jesus' entrance into Jerusalem. Willingly and with full knowledge of possible consequences, he chose to enter that place of death to bring us to life. Without rebelling or turning back, we must also choose a similar entrance.

It is a crucial, cross-shadowed, choice. Real feelings come into play. Frightening actions are to be taken. It means continually learning how to forgive and become ever more "for-giving." Choosing means refusing to shield our faces from buffets and spitting as well as giving our back to those who beat us and our cheeks to those who pluck our beard. Neither is pleasant. Both demand faith's fiery fervor.

This kind of living surfaces a truth none of us can easily embrace. Mockery, scoffing, scorn, and wagging heads will plague us. We will hear the jeers of unbelievers. "He...she...they...relied on the Lord. Let the Lord deliver them. Let the Lord rescue them, if the Lord loves them."

This is the hard fact—choosing God and goodness provokes rejection by those who refuse to make that decision.

No doubt you have struggled severely with the feelings effected by that radical choice. I know that I have. I do not appreciate being rejected. I do not enjoy being different when it brings alienation from those whom I like and love. Fear and distress are not easy to swallow.

Even less palatable is the personal angst that pursues me when I have deserted the Lord and fled. It is then that I learn that my choice does not guarantee instant, constant success. Nor will yours. Instead, we are allowed the grace of failure so that God might succeed through us. We are permitted the power of anguished screams—"My God, my God, why have you abandoned me?"

To choose God is to feel an immense sense of desolation, a complete voiding of self. Willingly taking the form of a slave, humbling ourselves, obediently accepting even death—just as Jesus did—we finally recognize truth. Discovering who we are and who we are becoming, we see where we have failed and where we are growing. Now, we have the audacity to dare to be as different as the woman who broke the alabaster jar of expensive perfume. In the action of taking that aromatic nard and pouring it extravagantly over Jesus' head, she offered him a generous gift—herself!

When we express our love in that manner, the earth quakes. The rocks of a previously pallid existence are split. Tombs of deadening apathy open. Those who keep watch are struck with awe at the passion they witness. From deep within them their witness of the powerful paradox discovered in palm-waving passion surges into speech. Fearfully, tremblingly, they declare,

"Truly these are the sons and daughters of God."

For Reflection and Discussion

- In what ways have you experienced being a sign of contradiction? When have you witnessed that truth in others? Where have you seen spiritually weary people? Describe specific ways in which you can speak a word that will rouse them. What comes to mind when you read the statement, "We are a passion people whose view of life is 'cross-eyed, but clear'"?

Prayer

Jesus, my brother, savior, and friend, I hold my palm branches high as I watch your triumphal entry into the Jerusalem of my life. I like the excitement of a parade, the fun and frolic of being one in a crowd of believers. I do not want to know that those waving branches will soon be replaced by the raising of the cross on Calvary's hill. Come to me now, as I hold those branches high, and grace me with a love for life lived at depth. Speak to me a word that will rouse me from my weariness and help me to attend to it. This I pray with all the passion of my heart. Amen.

Season of Easter

Easter Sunday

Acts 10:34, 37–43; Colossians 3:1–4; John 20:1–9

Rising from emptiness

Sometimes resurrection seems to be an impossibility. Bereft of our dearest friends, our prize possessions, and perhaps our health, we begin to feel like empty tombs blocked by boulders too large to be moved. It is quite difficult to process or progress from those Good Friday experiences and emotions without time for graceful grieving. Swift, smooth movement into celebratory Easter alleluias are often too much, too soon. We need a period of reminiscing—remembering in order to be re-membered. We need to give ourselves time to recall our history, newly integrating its details and weaving them into a tapestry of love. We need to ease ourselves into the rising from emptiness because we are "already-but-not-yet" Easter people who still cling to the comfortableness associated with recognized suffering.

However, we must be clear. There is nothing wrong with suffering—only the clinging to it.

Rising to life in Christ is costly. It is the priceless gift that impels us to set our hearts on what pertains to higher realms and asks us to "set your minds on things that are above, not on things that are on earth" (Col 3:2). When we truly allow ourselves to be resurrected, when we leave our tombs and enter the process involved in rising from emptiness, we also begin to live as Christ.

Jesus of Nazareth accepted his anointing with God's powerfully holy spirit and went about doing good works and healing all who were in the grip of evil. Intent on the will of God, Jesus surfaced the holiness deep in the things of earth. His human authenticity exposed the falseness found in blind adherence to legalism and set free the spirit of the law. In him, divinity and humanity embraced with creative, transforming love. To witness to the power of divinity working in humanity, we must be equally receptive and responsive.

Rising from emptiness means empowering others to a similar resurrection.

I am fortunate enough to belong to an interdenominational group of ministers who meet weekly to discuss the readings from the common lectionary. Usually we are a garrulous group. Each member comes armed with the result of personal reflection on the Word of God. All are ready and eager to expound on their viewpoint as well as to revel in the revelations received from the others. Pen scratchings can be heard as insights find their way onto pads of paper and are committed to mind and heart—ultimately to be preached. However, every once in a while, the Scriptures send us into profound silence. They intersect with our lives in ways both powerful and mysterious.

At times, it is an arabesque of irony that leaves us breathlessly graced. Those are the moments when we have come to the table feeling empty and impotent. Words of wisdom escape us. No help is found in quoting scholars. We are all left in speechless wonder—in vacant tombs.

It was on one of those occasions that I witnessed the potent gift of resurrection. Each minister had a different, equally hurtful experience to share with the only group that would truly be able to listen, hold the information in strict confidentiality, understand and resonate with the story. Minutes passed. The Sunday Scriptures were untouched while we remained, in company, under the cloud.

Or were they??

The stories are the story. The empty tomb must become *our* empty tomb, else resurrection cannot happen. And so it did. Early on that morning, while all of us were still in the dark, a woman present in the room of our sepulcher declared that prayer was needed to make sense of the continuing crucifixion. Quickly one of the men affirmed her statement and each member gave voice to the God within—and thus gave courage to those who could now receive the grace they had been dispensing but could not refill. Though her given name is Martha, she was the Magdalene who saw what the rest of us were yet unable to notice. The stone had been moved in the "mourning" darkness of that "first day." Once empty tombs, we were now filled with a rising spirit.

No one's problems had disappeared. Even the pain remained, diminished, not withdrawn. But the winding cloths had been removed. We were no longer bound by them, nor held tightly in death's grip. Each person in the room was graced to know the presence of God in a new and different way. This little community of believers came to the tomb of death, peered in, saw that Christ was not to be found in that place—and believed!

Christ has risen from the empty tomb. We, the people of God, are now rising from our own emptiness to be filled with the goodness we had squandered in trade for grandeur. Empowered by our resurrection we go forth to be Easter people to a Good Friday world. We are commissioned by our rising from the dead to preach and bear witness that all who believe in Christ are forgiven of their sins through his name. We are to be new yeast making fresh dough, leavening the bread of life with love. Sincerity and truth in the face of hypocrisy and lies are already both challenge and comfort to lives laid low by the pious platitudes of the religiously unreal.

Our Easter alleluias explode from a well of sorrow. Lashed with Good Friday thorns, they are inextricably entwined with the passion of the cross. Suffering does not diminish the glory of our song. It provides the counterpoint for an emerging harmony. To taste emptiness is to give zest to rising spirits and bring passion to the melody of our humanity. It gives new meaning to the words, "Let us rise...to pray."

For Reflection and Discussion

- How have you clung tightly to suffering lest resurrection be too frightening for you? What are the tombs in which you have interred your life, the winding cloths that keep you bound tightly in death's grip? Who is the Mary Magdalene in your life—the person who pronounces that the stone has been moved from your burial place? How have you been that person for others?

Prayer

Easter God of power and might,
You who removed every fear and fright,
Release me from my winding cloth each day
Take the stone that blocks my way
And place it far from me, I pray.
Let me see my empty tomb;
And know that life is yet my womb.
Grant me courage, strength, and sight
To make of darkness, blinding light.
Guide me on the path you choose
That I may always share Good News
Call me forth to be your disciple true
To walk and talk the Way with you.
Amen.

Do not look for Jesus among the dead!

Everything about Easter shouts a singular message: "Do not look for Jesus among the dead!" To seek Jesus among the living is a messy process often plagued with problems. There is a fearsome ebb and flow to vitality that brings suffering into the search and tests the genuineness of faith.

In the reading from the Acts of the Apostles, we are presented with an ideal gathering of Christian believers. With faith in full bloom, they are single-minded and determinedly enthusiastic. Their ardor is clear and well delineated. "They devoted themselves to the apostles' teaching and fellowship, to the breaking of bread and the prayers" (Acts 2:42).

A marvelous and awesome unity marked the group. Togetherness required holding all things in common, even to the extent of selling property and possessions, dividing them among all according to each one's need. Remarkably, this was a daily experience of discernment and radical Christianity. Teaching and learning, living and listening, praising and thanking were not options but commitments to the belief that Jesus could not, would not, be found among the dead. Valuable, necessary signs of commitment then, they are no less essential today.

There is another side to the Christian life, however, that also pervades through the ages. It is our persistence in the search for Jesus among the dead. Looking for Jesus among the living is a demanding vocation that necessitates vital vulnerability and surfaces fear! It is much more comfortable, though far less comforting, to seek Jesus among the dead who neither offer nor ask for challenge. Worse yet is the way of the living dead who follow the maxim: Don't ask, don't tell, don't live, don't die—be apathetic!

In contrast to the ardently unified community of faith described in the Acts of the Apostles, the one mentioned in the gospel according to John is arduously uniform in their common fear of reprisal. By this time, Christian believers had been forcibly separated from their Jewish roots. It was a scary time for those who sought to expand life as well as those who wished to contain and maintain the past, locking out change or modification.

Even those known to be disciples felt this terror. Like us, they were weakly human men and women. Their belief was tempered by reality. Perhaps weakness drew them together rather than strength. They may have known that Jesus was not to be sought among the dead, but were hoping that he would be found among the "dying." Indecisive, wondering, frightened people, they joined as one for the solace revealed in community.

And so, the Jesus who could not be sought among the dead did, in fact, come to those who cowered at living and were afraid of dying. In the midst of their unholy fear, Jesus came to them and offered them wholeness. "Peace, be with you" he said—showing them the wounds of authenticity.

Jesus, the wounded healer, commissions his disciples to follow in his way. We are to go where people cower in the midst of their fear and show them our wounds. With them we are to discover where peace of faith may be found—in the touching forgiveness of a forgiving touch.

There will always be those who cannot believe what we have seen and experienced. In reality, these "doubting Thomases" are gifts to believers. They ground the community in honesty. They are the ones who chance ridicule yet speak their truth. Frequently, they give voice to feelings others keep carefully, silently hidden.

These are the believers who overtly express their need to see the Lord as they can—not as others have! There is such a contrast drawn between those who had excitedly exclaimed their vision of the Lord yet continued to securely lock their doors and Thomas who artlessly proclaimed his doubt. I am always struck by the genuineness of the "doubters" I meet along the way. Unafraid to risk divine disfavor with their truth, they are graced by God's presence and believe ever more deeply. Like Thomas, their exclamation—"My Lord and my God"—is a powerfully profound expression of total commitment.

Thomas provides a model for all whose faith is forged in a crucible of doubt. We who are questioners refuse to proclaim belief only to barricade the doors of faith with obstacles of fear. Instead, we sally forth into the desert of unknowing, readying ourselves, or being readied, for blind faith with sighted eyes.

Thomas the Doubter became the Apostle of Daring, especially for his companions in the community of faith. He exemplified the power inherent in facing unbelief and permitting the embrace of belief. Where once he had professed a need to touch Jesus and put his hands into those sacred wounds, now Thomas understood that touching was not enough. He had to be touched by the power of God's spirit. He had to be sent, as a wounded healer, to the disconsolate—and he had to go to them by the way of the cross where they were hanging, expectantly.

We modern-day Thomases are no less dense regarding the lengths to which Jesus will go to ensure our faith. Jesus gives us vibrant believers to help unlock the doors of our fear. He places them right in the middle of our confusion and doubt. Wounded healers, they offer hope in the company of saints. By example and in ways relevant to modern living, they teach us how to be a people united in devoted love for God and each other—people who do not look for Jesus among the dead.

For me, Thomas Merton unravels both the mystery of Jesus' appearance to the disciples and complications of community living. Merton tells us to dare to "discover what we already have. Start where you are. Deepen what you already have. Realize you are already there. We now have everything, but we don't know it, and we don't experience it. Everything has been given to us in Christ. All we need is to experience what we really possess." Embrace the doubters' hurt, the hurting doubt. Experience the healing touch of peace in the midst of fear. Share all that you are. Become the devoted people of God.

Above all, do not look for Jesus among the dead.

For Reflection and Discussion

- What is your response/reaction/experience of the statement: "To seek Jesus among the living is a messy process often plagued with problems"? When have you been a Doubting Thomas? How did that affect your personal spirituality and that of your family and/or faith community? In what specific ways can you deepen who you are and come to realize that everything has already been given to us in Christ?

Prayer

Dear God, so often I doubt my own ability to be Christlike. I do not want to expose my vulnerability and frailty. I fear that someone will want to put a finger into my wounds, probing them and causing me pain. I even question if my faith will emerge stronger and purer from this crucible of doubt. So, I look for Jesus among the empty tombs of my own deadliness. Help me to know that Jesus is among the living, the questioners, the believers, even among those who have locked the doors of their hearts in fearfulness. Help me to know that Jesus lives in me. Let me pray, "My Lord and my God!" Amen.

THIRD SUNDAY OF EASTER

ACTS 2:14, 22–33; I PETER 1:17–21; LUKE 24:13–35

Walking down the wrong aisle, talking

One day my sister was busily discussing with me all that had happened in her young daughter's life. She was engaged in a lively monologue of maternal advice and suggestions as I listened with the heart and ears of an older sibling who had been that route many years before. Neither of us noticed that we were not alone in the room, until a small voice interrupted our reverie. I smiled as I heard my niece tell her Mom, "You are walking down the wrong aisle, talking."

With the limited vocabulary and worldview of a four year old, Crista was calmly but emphatically stating that her mother was a person who just didn't get it. At that moment, my sister was, as far as her daughter was concerned, someone who did not understand what was happening right before her own eyes. Crista noticed that her mom was talking bunches of words without recognizing reality. What amazed me was that Crista saw life with her Mom as Jesus experienced life with his disciples on that Emmaus road so long ago.

Struck by the similarity, I realize how often I find myself walking that same Emmaus road. I really believe I have a handle on things, such as life, religion, Jesus. I really think I am in touch with the meaning of Christianity: the cross, passionate suffering, intense love. I study and meditate, ponder and contemplate. Then I discuss, share, and teach what I have learned and experienced. But, the fact is that I am still talking, talking, talking! And probably protesting far too much!

My journey takes me away from Jerusalem's sorrow, hurrying to put that sadness behind me because I do not understand it, nor do I wish to participate in its pain. My words betray me. Filled with fading hope and waning optimism, I echo the remarks of Cleopas and his companion. Like them, I also was "hoping that Jesus was the one who would set me free." As they felt that nothing had changed, despite the crucifixion and resurrection, so, at times, do I! All their hopes were pinned on an impoverished image of a victorious Messiah. So are mine! This Jesus who promises much seems to deliver so little. Called to friendship, I still feel enslaved and powerless.

Resurrection appears limited to the emptiness of a tomb. What is wrong?

Too small minds have contrived a too small God.

We seek freedom as we know it; victory on our terms. As a result, we remain bound. Here I am, still chained to my own limited interpretation of love and constrained by self-centeredness.

My behavior fits Crista's judgment: I am walking down the wrong aisle, talking!

The absolute wonder of it all is that Jesus is walking down the same aisle. He approaches me. He makes the first move and begins to walk with me. Involved in my private angst and analysis, I do not recognize him. Busy in my interpretation of events that have caused pain, isolation, alienation, even death, I need a jolt. I need something, someone, to stem the incessant talking and start the listening process. I need a Crista to remind me that I am walking down the wrong aisle, talking!

For each of us, there is such a person. There is someone who tells us how little sense we have, how slow we are to believe. Ours is a pilgrimage through a strange world filled with an interminable flood of words. It is arduous and dotted with obstacles that keep us from being still and knowing God. We need—and are given—a companion sojourner to support and challenge us as we journey through the noisiness of thoughts and ideas, judgments and evaluations.

Ceaselessly, the sound of words pervades, destroying the silence of quiet companionship with God. Even our prayers are often too wordy. They are a swirling, whirling, twirling cyclone of feelings we think God needs to hear. While we jabber, Jesus stays and waits—a steady, tranquil presence. Trying to let us know who he is, he does all in his power to show us hope in the heart of hopelessness, light in the face of darkness, love in the midst of fear. Jesus is our deliverer. He is the one who remains to the very end of our days so that we shall not be disturbed. Jesus is the Promise who never dies or changes. The Christ who is our Easter shows us the paths of life and fills us with joy. No endless talking here—simply example.

One of the greatest lessons offered to believers is found in the Emmaus story: we learn to be wayfarers by being in the way. En route to Emmaus, the disciples are open-eyed only after experiencing Jesus as the God-man who sits down with us to eat. Similarly, the blinders drop from our eyes. Our vision is made clear and focused when we sit down together to share the table meal of life.

When we take the bread, the very substance, of our existence, bless it, proclaim its goodness, and return it to our Creator God, we are learning to be Jesus. Awareness does not come until we break into the crustiness to unveil our soft interior now open for sharing with others. In the sacredness of that revelation, we are made free to recognize Christ! In that same moment, Christ disappears—leaving us to be Christ for each other. Only then do we begin to touch the mystery, the truth, of resurrection.

When I break my heart, my very being, for you—and you do the same for me—when our vulnerable selves are shared, we know God. We touch love. Crosses melt into "Son-rises."

No longer do I walk down the wrong aisle, talking. I do not walk away from Jerusalem's passion, blinded by a westward journey into sunset. I see the Lord ever before me and I am not disturbed. I dwell in hope because the paths of life have been made known to me.

I am an Easter Christian sojourning into the Son-rise. And my heart is burning within me!

For Reflection and Discussion

- Who do you need and want to be walking down your Emmaus road with you? What are the reasons for that choice or those choices? Describe a time or two when you have made God too small, or when others have diminished God for you. What is your experience of journeying into the Son-rise?

Prayer

God in heaven, author of all truth, a people once in darkness has listened to your Word and followed your Son as he rose from the tomb. Hear the prayer of this newborn people and strengthen your Church to answer your call. may we rise and come forth into the light of day to stand in your presence until eternity dawns. We ask this through our Lord Jesus Christ, your Son, who lives and reigns with you and the Holy Spirit, one God for ever and ever. Amen.

—Alternative Opening Prayer, Third Sunday of Easter

ACTS 2:14, 36–41; 1 PETER 2:20–25; JOHN 10:1–10

Beyond the shadow of doubt

So often we have allowed doubt to cast a shadow on our faith. We let it tinge credence with incredulity, casting the gloom of uncertainty upon the grace of certitude—causing distress and dismay to dog our steps and burden our spirits. We are shaken, but not to the core. To try to dismiss doubt summarily, banishing it to the darkest corner we can find, does no good. Somehow it surfaces when we least suspect and we are, once again, ill at ease.

I would suspect that, instead of dismissal, we need to confront doubt head-on. We need to go beyond the shadow of doubt and enter its darkness. We need to let it shake us to the deepest, most central, part of our being—and ask the age-old question of disciples: "What should we do, brothers and sisters…what should we do?" (Acts 2:37).

The answer is simply profound and startlingly serious. Our task, our vocation, the goal of our life is to re-form ourselves into Jesus, the Christ, be baptized into his name, and allow the holiness of his spirit to gift us with new life. If we refuse, if we do not enter Christ's sheepfold through the gate of radical change and try, instead, to climb in another way, we are no less than thieves and marauders!

What a harsh message! It even seems to shout exclusivity when Christianity is called to be a religion of universality—until we take a second and closer look. That inspection reveals a radical inclusivity. Once the "shepherd of the sheep" entered the gate of humanity and reopened it to critical presence of divinity, only he, only the Messiah of humanity, is the gatekeeper. Only the Christ can command or reject admission!

Contrary to most gatekeepers whose task is to keep people out, Christ seeks their entry. He wishes to attain and maintain an intimate, personal relationship with those who are his. Like a shepherd who tends his flock day and night, in good weather and ill, Jesus the Christ "calls his own sheep by name and leads them out" (Jn 10:3).

Christ does the calling—and the counting and the leading! Our sole—our soul's—task is to go beyond the shadow of doubt and find the substance of

God's dominion. The only "leading" we need to worry about is that which comes through following.

In my parochial school youth, the sisters always admonished, "When in doubt, don't." Their advice was sound for young people who are not yet honed in the sacrificial fires of wisdom. As we make our choices and grow in "whole-iness," we also learn to recognize God's voice in the midst of all doubt. We learn not to follow the call of a stranger—no matter how enticing or pietistic the invitation may be.

My daughter recently told me about a difficult situation that challenged her parenting skills. As I listened to her story, I heard maternal words of wisdom—as well as the anguish beneath them. I heard the voice of a mother who was trying her very best to be the sheepgate for her child. She asked her daughter to remember always the feeling in her heart that came when evil doubts tried to rob her goodness. "Remember that feeling in your heart," she said, "and never do what that feeling tells you not to do." In her own way, she was telling her little one to be attentive to the voice you recognize—the voice of God residing in you—and flee quickly from the strange sounds of all who would do you harm.

Go beyond the shadow of doubt—and find life.

This is the process of a lifetime. It requires our putting up with suffering for doing what is right. In fact, it calls for such passion. We are in a line of martyrs that stretches back to Christ and forward to eternity. Christ suffered for us in this way and asked that we follow in his footsteps. "'He committed no sin, and no deceit was found in his mouth.' When he was abused, he did not return abuse; when he suffered, he did not threaten; but he entrusted himself to the one who judges justly" (1 Pt 2:22–23).

There is no doubt about the Christian lifestyle. There are no shadowy places to hide or pretend. In full Sonlight, dimness vanishes. All is seen clearly. So, Christians are people who do no wrong. They speak without deceit in their mouths or hearts. When insulted, they return no insult. Nor do they counter any suffering with threats or desire for retribution. Instead, the people of God deliver themselves up to the One who judges justly—and pay no heed to those who demand vengeance and desire injustice.

Jesus modeled the Way for all to go beyond doubt's shadows to find love, light, life, and truth. As it was not easy for him, so shall it not be easy for us. However, we have the assurance of his lead, and need no longer wander in the wilderness. At one time, we were straying like sheep looking for pasture in dangerous places. Uncertainty plagued us. Now we know that salvation rests upon our return to the shepherd. In him, with him, and through him, we are secure and safe. He will find the best place for us to feed. He will do the foraging for us. We have only to enter through him, follow, and be fed.

Going beyond the shadow of doubt brings us to the shalom of sanctity. There we taste and see how good God is. There we realize the divine presence that has always been with us. Going beyond the shadow of doubt is re-creative. It takes all fantasy out of faith and sharpens it to a faithful edge. Going beyond the shadow of doubt allows us to rest in the wonder that "goodness and mercy shall follow me all the days of my life, and I shall dwell in the house of the Lord my whole life long" (Ps 23:6).

When we continue going beyond the shadow of doubt we achieve what Christ came into our world to accomplish. We have life—and have it to the full.

For Reflection and Discussion

- What examples can you give of times when you have patiently suffered for doing what is good? How were those experiences "graces before God?" What is the name God has given you, the name by which God calls you?

Prayer

Dear God, I hear the words of a hymn echoing in my mind. I want to sing it over and over again, for I need you to, "Shepherd me, O God, beyond my wants, beyond my fears, from death into life." I need you to guard the gate of my humanity from the marauders of my own making. I need you to protect me from the deadly enemies of pride and prejudice, anger and anguish, greed and gluttony that I carry inside my secret self. Alone, I am helpless and fall prey to my failings. With you as the gateway to my truest self, I can do all things. So, I beg again: "Shepherd me, O God, beyond my wants, beyond my fears, from death into life." Amen.

—Hymn text by Marty Haugen ©1986, GIA Publications

FIFTH SUNDAY OF EASTER

ACTS 6:1–7; 1 PETER 2:4–9; JOHN 14:1–12

Left behind

A few years ago there was a wild rush to read the Left Behind series written by Tim LaHaye. Written in novel form, the books gave a modern twist to the ancient writings of the Book of Revelation. Churches held educational sessions and discussion groups based on LaHaye's works. Advocates and critics alike paid attention to the message, trading opinions and offering scholarly alternatives. No matter which side of the argument was taken, one reality emerged—people were hooked.

Who…why…where…when…for how long are people left behind? What is "being left behind"? These are interesting questions to ponder in the light of Scripture. Who did Jesus leave behind? Why? Where were/are the "left-behind-ers"? When and for how long are we to be left behind?

In reality, we are all among those whom Jesus left behind, if we have chosen to be disciples. Our mission and commission are to be living stones in the edifice of Christianity. Stable, rock-hard in radical determination and conviction, we are also alive and dynamically vital to its essence. Disciples are people who adhere to the tradition of God's word and move in harmony with its creative inspiration. Disciples are those Jesus left behind to continue the redemptive work begun in his incarnation and brought to completion, but not conclusion, in his passion, death, and resurrection.

The work of discipleship is both simple and complicated. Its simplicity stems from grounded faith in God. Therefore, disciples are not troubled people. Its complexity derives from the fact that God's house has many dwelling places. There is a particular room prepared for each of us. We are set aside, as individuals and in community, for a unique mission and ministry. In God's image and likeness we were created. In that same image, we are to be divinely human reflections of the multifaceted jewel we call "the word of God."

This is the task of a lifetime.

From early on, the people of God have had to deal with complaints and criticism. Disciples were not exempt. They soon recognized their limitations—and the problems that derived from those restrictions. Neglect became an issue. Those who were left behind had to address the fact that all were equally called to different service. They could not leave a wake of negligence trailing their eagerness to share the gospel message.

Quickly it became apparent that nothing must deter praying, integrating, and ministering within God's word. At the same time, they noted that no one can hear God's word while physical needs distracted them. Somehow, both word and work must be shared. Hierarchical arrangements, thank God, were not the first consideration—except to note that ecclesial "hierarchy" is the one that best effects service to and with the vulnerable people of God. Those with spiritual, physical, psychological, and emotional needs must be our prime consideration. First and foremost, Jesus of Nazareth lived, worked, preached, and was present to those who were vulnerable. The Word of God spoke the word of God to people in need. God's people—disciples—can do no less.

If doing good things interferes with being good people, if activity demeans the action of the gospel message and brings death to the vitality of living stones, we must change the situation. Christianity is a "both/and" religion. Both word and work are equally necessary. We are not talking about the establishment of a liturgical or ecclesial hierarchy of the ordained. The issue at hand is comprehension of what it means to be the Body of Christ, what it means to be housekeepers in a mansion comprised of many dwelling places. It is not so much that we follow the advice of Lin Yutang, who says, "Besides the noble art of getting things done, there is the noble art of leaving things undone. The wisdom of life consists in the elimination of non-essentials." It is that we recognize what is essential and seek creative accomplishment.

The people of God must pray together to discern the presence and appropriate use of God-given talents and gifts, both individual and communal, offered that we might meet obvious and pressing needs. We are presenting and being presented with the necessity of a community grounded in deep spirituality and profound prudence.

Though we cannot return to the days of the early church, we are able to learn from its successes and failures. When facing the dilemma of dissension among the disciples, specifically regarding perceived injustices, the community gathered for prayerful discussion. The injustice was named, "It is not right that we should neglect the word of God in order to wait on tables" (Acts 6:2). A possible solution was proposed. "Therefore, friends, select from among yourselves seven men of good standing, full of the Spirit and of wisdom, whom we may appoint to this task, while we, for our part, will devote ourselves to prayer and to serving the word" (Acts 6:3–4).

The solution was not nearly as important as the fact that it was unanimously accepted. The body of Christ was in complete agreement that each member had a unique and equally essential role to play in the life of Christ. The church needs all of us, whether sacramentally ordained or not. The edifice would crumble without its living stones. All shapes and sizes are vital. Each fits into a specific niche to keep the construction intact and viable.

God has created a place for each of us—both here and in the hereafter. In that place we come to understand our personal relationship with the God who lives in us, accomplishing what God wishes to have done. It is the way of truth and life created for us, alone and together. It is the path to providence made for "a chosen race, a royal priesthood, a holy nation, God's own people, in order that you may proclaim the mighty acts of him who called you out of darkness into his marvelous light" (1 Pt 2:9).

Yes, we have been left behind to do faithfully the works of Christ—and far greater than these!

For Reflection and Discussion

- What specific words and works have you been left behind to accomplish? What giftedness do you possess that empowers your task? How can you be both a minister of the word and a table servant in your family? Among your friends? At your workplace? In your home? In your faith community?

Prayer

Fill me with faith and your Spirit of Wisdom, O God. Let me learn to live as one left behind so that I can be your eyes and ears, arms and legs to a world always awaiting redemption. I thank you for the gifts you have given me, gifts that empower me and give me the courage to live as a member of the Body of Christ. Help me never to neglect your word as I work to surface your kingdom. Help me never to avoid your work as I listen, pray, and share your word. Be with me, O God, as I strive to be present to others. And never let me be a stumbling block, an obstacle in the path of all who journey with me en route to our eternal home. Amen.

SIXTH SUNDAY OF EASTER

ACTS 8:5–8, 14–17; 1 PETER 3:15–18; JOHN 14:15–21

The advocate of truth

"I will ask the Father, and he will give you another Advocate, to be with you forever. This is the Spirit of truth, whom the world cannot receive" (Jn 14:16–17).

As we draw closer to Pentecost, we are also drawn more deeply into the mystery of Christianity. The presence of God in love and truth is more evident, as is the challenge for Christians to be lovers of truth and justice. Christians are emphatically Easter people who speak the truth of justice in love. Resurrection is our cry. However, resurrection glory and peace come via the pain and passion of Good Friday, endured with the inspiration and courage of our Advocate God who is always with us.

The paraclete of truth dwells in an abode of love and hope. The paraclete of truth is found where there is life—and life is revealed when we authentically mediate honesty. Many claim to be pro-life but find it difficult to recognize life when it requires sacrificial dying. They do not really want to get close enough to life to impose hands on it and receive the holiness of its spirit. Life in the Spirit of God asks that we become transparent people—open and not opaque, vulnerable in our virtue. Life in the Spirit of God leads us beyond the veil of acceptance and makes us unrecognizable to all who see only what the world sees—success, power, money, prestige, status, upward mobility.

To live in and with the paraclete of truth in our heart of hearts is to venerate only Christ. It is to find reason for hope solely in God. God can do nothing until we respond in love to his love for us. The way that we can determine if we are indeed a loving people is by examining our obedience to God's commands. There is nothing complicated here. Nor is it an easy way to live!

Its simplicity lies solely in the reality that love is obedience to God alone—to no one and nothing else. Only when we lovingly obey God's command, God's call, are we truly alive, radically and magnificently free. Only then can we recognize Jesus, the Spirit of Truth. "In a little while the world will no longer see me, but you will see me; because I live, you also will live. On that day you will know that I am in my Father, and you in me, and I in you" (Jn 14:19–20). That's the holy family. Christ in the Father, we in Christ, Christ in us!

Words and explanations, analyzing and theologizing—all of which are good and necessary—can sometimes be used to complicate the experience. So can the "too easy path" of simplistic belief that ignores the need to try to probe the mystery. Virtue always lies in the middle path: faith seeking to understand while living the questions.

Peter—the great homilist and simple, outspoken fisherman—had it all put together. Obedience to God's commands meant soul-deep hope and equally integrated truth. This was then, and is for us now, his repeated message. Deeply rooted, this hope is the radical refusal to set limits. No limits are placed on God's action in us; none on our action in, through, and with God.

To hope in God is to let God loose! Unchain the God we hold bound. Let God save us from ourselves. Allow God to take away our inadequacies and empower us to cope with life and truth. Permit God to make us fit to see as God wants us to see. It is true, you know, that we see things not as they are, but as we are. That means we all need continuing re-creation in order to be revisionists. This is not theological jargon. Something quite extraordinary occurred when the first Christians lived in radical hope with the Paraclete of Truth. Healing happened. Joy filled their lives. They were noticed because they were different—a ray of sunshine in a darkened, hopeless world; life amid the web of death.

Real then, it is real now. There is an extraordinary "every-day-ness" about Christianity that makes it available, practical, observable, and believable. Again, it is Peter who gives us the manual for Christian living. First of all, "venerate Christ in your hearts." Begin at the only spot we can: our own hearts. Trust that Christ is already there and live accordingly. Be the living tabernacles we are—each and all of us. Remember those living stones that were mentioned earlier in 1 Peter (2:5)? Here we are—the building blocks of Christianity.

When we live reverently in hope, sooner or later someone is going to note our vitality and ask questions. Just as was true for those first Christians, who we are speaks louder than anything we have to say. However, once the question is asked, we need to be ever ready to reply and give reason for this hope of ours. Know who we are. Know who God is. Do, as Peter cautions, speak "with gentleness and reverence" (1 Pet 3:16). Follow the example of Jesus. Never force or coerce. Wait patiently for others. Walk with them; pray with them. Reverence where others are. Respect and honor their truth, remembering that hoping in God is trusting that God refuses to set limits.

The spirit of truth sustains us. Truth will never leave us orphans. Always, in one way or another, a member of God's family will come to us in our need to support, encourage, give hope, and bolster faith. Because the family lives, each of us lives. More and more—the older we grow—we identify with each other. We see ourselves in each other, both in faith and in foibles.

Surprises will happen. People will be placed on our path to learn the Way. We will be placed in the Way of others. Together we will be transformed. Together we will learn to recognize the divinity who lives in us. Together we will receive the Holy Spirit, the Paraclete of Truth, already given to us. Together we will be, become, and celebrate our call to holiness and wholeness. Together we will know that we are not orphans. We are saints.

We are people whose life makes it easier to believe in God because we are paracletes of truth, listening to each other in love so that we might continue to speak the truth of justice with love.

For Reflection and Discussion

- What did you experience when you last spoke the truth of justice in love? How did you feel? Who was the audience and what was the response/reaction? In what ways can our "listening with love" be enhanced and intensified? What did you experience when you have been the recipient of truth spoken with love?

Prayer

Spirit of Truth, God of Wisdom, Light, and Love, come into my heart and mind that I might be empowered to listen with love and speak the truth of justice with love. Let me stand in the fires of compassionate under-standing and burn with the desire to surface your presence in this world of ours. Let me take, receive, and integrate your spirit of truth. Gently, reverently, may I bask in the hope of resurrection—and share that hope with all who enter my life. Amen.

THE FEAST OF THE ASCENSION

ACTS 1:1–11; EPHESIANS 1:17–32; MATTHEW 28:16–20

Movin' on up to a deluxe apartment in the sky

For a number of years, television audiences enjoyed the antics of Archie Bunker, his wife, daughter, son-in-law, and neighbors. His overt prejudices revealed an ignorance shared but hidden in the lives of everyday folks like you and me. The canned laughter gave little evidence of the mixed emotions that ran through the real-life families who were watching—groups of people who struggled mightily, or not at all, with the discomfort they felt when faced with their own concretized opinions and callous outrage.

Archie represented the low middle-class America of his day. He could not understand how his black neighbor, George, could succeed while he—loyalist, law-abiding Archie Bunker—remained in a stolid status quo, ensconced in his well-worn easy chair. How could a black man who owned a cleaners be the chosen one? How could he be "movin' on up"?

For his part, George saw ascendancy as being power, prestige, and position for himself and his wife Louise (Weezie). He delighted in the opportunity to use this move as a weapon against the Archie Bunkers of the world and as an instrument to enter the caste of the upper crust. Ascension meant upward mobility. It demanded distance from a disdainful past, detachment from all that could taint progress, and deliberate entry into the good life. George was well prepared to comply, despite the protests of his wife who had a different sense of life's reality.

And so we laughed at his and Archie's loud protestations and buffoonery. We laughed despite ourselves. Truth be told, our apparent growth and enlightenment over the years belies the fact that little change has actually occurred.

For most of us, ascension still means that we are somehow "movin' on up to a deluxe apartment in the sky."

That meaning colors our religious beliefs as well as our social and economic status. We remain stuck, as were the disciples, standing in place and looking intently at the sky to find a clouded Jesus being taken from our sight. We seek a heavenly hereafter at the price of the divine incarnation to be found on earth in all creation. We ignore the Christ who is in our search for the Christ who will be. We look to the time when we'll move on up to a land of milk and honey where there are no tears or mourning. Unhappily in the process, we neither recognize nor realize the ascension that occurs in our spirit here and now.

Blinded to that reality, we forget the reason we are here. We forget the reason that Jesus the Christ chose to become one of us. We forget that the power of ascendancy lies within us as inspirited human beings—people endowed with and baptized into the indomitable, holy spirit of God. That is our ascension, our resurrection, and our eternal life.

We can live this life anywhere and everywhere. We are neither bound by our precious armchairs nor our prestigious apartments. Gender, race, creed, culture are not deterrents. Whether free or imprisoned, we are urged to "lead a life worthy of the calling to which you have been called, with all humility and gentleness, with patience, bearing with one another in love, making every effort to maintain the unity of the Spirit in the bond of peace. There is one body and one Spirit, just as you were called to the one hope of your calling, one Lord, one faith, one baptism, one God and Father of all, who is above all and through all and in all" (Eph 4:1–6).

How we live our ascension is both gift and choice. Some of us have been given the grace to be apostles. Others may be prophets or evangelists, pastors and teachers. God is already movin' us on up to our deluxe apartment, but the abode is not to be discovered later in the sky above. God has selected and measured the space uniquely for us. It is ready for use right here, right now on this planet we occupy. This is the home in which we will attain the full stature of Christ!

Going to church on Sunday is not enough. Looking to the sky for God is not enough. Skimming the surface of life is not enough. Remaining stuck in an armchair existence is not enough nor is residing in affluent ascendancy. We have a call to hear and heed.

We will understand the meaning of ascension when we go into the whole world and proclaim the gospel to every creature. That does not mean that each of us will have to don a missionary's robe and run to find a pagan somewhere who could be converted. It does mean that each of us must find and convert the pagan unbeliever who lives in our own heart and home. Every bias and prejudice we harbor needs to be unveiled, condemned, and destroyed. Every moment used for alienation, isolation, exclusion needs to be converted to a time of acceptance, embrace, and inclusion. We need to drive out our own demons before we address those of others.

Each of us must continually baptize ourselves with God's spirit of love. We must incarnate our belief that God's good news is alive in all people. We must meet people where they are, honoring and revering them as they are not as we wish them to be. We must speak in new languages, universal tongues that tell of justice and truth, peace and freedom.

While we are ascending to those divine heights, we will also, without harm, be able to pick up the serpents of pride and prejudice, fear and frustration, anger and animosity, greed and gluttony. Fearlessly, we will demonstrate their powerlessness in the face of goodness. We will lay hands on the sick, and they will recover—not because of our holiness but in the graciousness of God who saves us from ourselves.

When we think of Ascension, we cannot be people who stand in the muck and mire of life, looking upward to a clouded Jesus in the sky above. We cannot be people who wait to see what God will do without ever entering into the being and action of incarnation.

Signs of God's existence are to be found in all creation. People of the Ascension need to attend to the God who works with us, within us, through us. We need to seek and see the signs by which God confirms the divine word of Christ through life in us.

Only then will we truly be on the Way, "movin' on up to the deluxe apartment in the sky!"

For Reflection and Discussion

- How do you plan to enter into the being and action of incarnation in specific ways this week? What signs of God have you seen in creation? How have those signs spoken to you? In what ways have you carried out everything God has commanded of you?

Prayer

Lord, teach me to pray and trust more fully in you. Give me assurance that you are with me always, and teach me to be content with the plan you have for me and all your creatures.

—*All Will Be Well*, Richard Chilson ©1995 Quest Associates

SEVENTH SUNDAY OF EASTER

ACTS 1:12–14; I PETER 4:13–16; JOHN 17:1–11

Go with the glow, not the flow

Readings from Scripture are frequently filled with references to glory and encased in an atmosphere of prayer. Prayer is somewhat familiar to us. At least the action of prayer is. We know how to say our prayers. Glory, however, remains a mystery.

Dictionaries are not tremendously helpful in our search for understanding, unless we skip down to the least known usage: "radiant beauty or splendor; magnificence; the bliss of heaven." Now we have a starting point! Taken from the perspective of radiance, magnificence, and bliss, both Peter's letter and the Johannine account of Jesus' farewell prayer are wonderfully consoling. "Happy are you when you are insulted for the sake of Christ, for then God's Spirit in its glory has come to rest on you," and "Father, give glory to your Son that your Son may give glory to you, that he may bestow eternal life on those you gave him."

If we were steeped in our Jewish heritage, we would immediately recognize the *shekinah* (presence of glory) associated with God. Unfortunately, in Christian art, we have stylized that sense of glorified presence into a halo—and limited it to Jesus and canonized saints. Happily we know, deep down, that halos are insufficient. God's glory is vital and dynamic. It is a living, lively presence that bubbles up as enthusiastic verve. We name it, perhaps unwittingly, when we describe the bride and groom as simply glowing or say that the pregnant woman is aglow. The television program, *Touched by An Angel*, announces angelic presence with a suffusing and effusing brightness that touches "ordinary" people with extraordinary awareness. Somehow we sense that the glow we see has something to do with life and love. It is the glory associated with God's presence in our lives.

We want and seek that glow. Commercials about cosmetics certainly attest to that as they lure us to blushes and "healthy" tans. New age religions speak of the auras people have. In either case, we miss the point entirely! The glow of God's presence in our lives happens when we are fully alive, as Irenaeus wrote. I saw it printed as a challenging question on the back of a T-shirt a youngster wore to church recently: "Do you want to die or are you just afraid to live?"

We are already called to that glory, that full life. It is our destiny to live as Jesus did, fully alive to each moment. It is our destiny to be people who believe in tomorrow while living today. *Carpe diem* is our call. Seize the day and all of its providence, finish the work God gives us to do.

As Jesus worked, so do we—to make God's name known to those God gives us in the world (see Jn 17:6–8). There is much labor in that vocation. It presupposes our own knowledge of God—a knowledge gained in and through constant devotion to prayer, both communal and individual. Jesus remained in prayer always, intensifying his prayerfulness before entering into any important challenges. His disciples, family, and friends followed that example. So must we. Pray always and in all ways.

Without this prayerful attentiveness to God's presence, the call and message of God will be both disabled and disarmed. Discernment will be impaired. Suffering will be misdirected and non-redemptive. Within a prayerful life we discover the joy experienced in suffering for being a Christian.

That sort of suffering is not something we eagerly anticipate; nor do we seek it out. I can remember learning a prayer that begged, "Blood flowing from the side of Christ, fill me with a love for suffering and sorrow for my sins." Though I pray it at the consecration of every Mass, I pray it fearfully. With a healthy trepidation, I am reminding God that "love" is not "like." I pray it knowing that I must; for suffering is part and parcel of passionate living. If I am to be fully alive, I shall not escape the passion. Christians cannot retreat from the world and busy themselves in a life removed from the rough and tumble of the everyday world. Jesus didn't.

Of course, there is a need of prayer and meditation and quiet times, times when we shut the door upon the world to be alone with God, but, they are the means to the end; and the end of life is to demonstrate the Christian life in the ordinary work of the world. Christianity was never meant to withdraw a man from life; it was meant to equip him better for life. Christianity does not offer us release from problems; it offers us a way to solve our problems. Christianity does not offer us a life in which troubles are escaped and evaded; it offers us a life in which troubles are faced and conquered....The Christian must never desire to abandon the world; he must always desire to win the world." (*The Gospel of John*, William Barclay)

Because we are called to win the world, Jesus prays for us, assuring our ultimate success. Strengthened in his prayerfulness, we find the courage to face the Jerusalems of our day. We are radical in our optimism and are empowered to believe that we shall see the good things of the Lord in the land of the living. Where people are fully alive the goodness of the Lord is also visible. There is an aura, a halo, a glow that emanates from the people of God.

The glow warms the cold of despair with its shimmering heat. It softens the hardness of hearts. It lights up the dark shadows of fear, exposing them to the bright clarity of faith. It heals the hurt and pain of persecution. It beckons, draws, impels all in its range to come home to God.

There is a vigor about God's people. There is a radiant beauty about us. To paraphrase the gospel according to John, "We are all God has left. We are a splendid people, a magnificent creation. We are the glory of Jesus." We are the people whose song and prayer is to rise and shine, and give God the glory! That is our cry. That is our call.

Our vocation is to go with the *glow*, not the flow!

For Reflection and Discussion

- How have you experienced the value and blessedness to be found in being "insulted for the sake of Christ?" In what ways has that "blessed suffering" brought you into deeper life? Give examples of times when you have been "touched by an angel," and times when you have been the "touching angel." How has prayer helped you to know God?

Prayer

Dearest God of shining glory, my deepest heart calls out for the shook foil of divinity. I want to rise and shine. I want to give you glory and bask in your light, love, and life. I come to you in trembling awe and wonder, a little frightened at the cost of discipleship. Let me not be afraid to live. Please let me feel the power of your presence and give me the strength to be a glowing sign of your radiant beauty, always and everywhere. I pray this petition in the name of Jesus, the Christ who lives and reigns with you and the Spirit forever. Amen.

PENTECOST SUNDAY

ACTS 2:1–11; 1 CORINTHIANS 12:3–7,12–13; JOHN 20:19–23

The dance of discipleship

As with all creation, there is movement in discipleship. It is not a static spot to stake and claim but a dynamic disposition to share and consecrate. There is a creative cycle to discipleship. From the early disciples who gathered in one place seeking the comfort of companionship behind locked doors to the present day, the followers of Christ move from fear to faith. In a spiraling pirouette, we enter the dance of discipleship, gathering ourselves together to scatter ourselves throughout the world. It is both progress and process with intertwining steps that sometimes entangle and often are indistinguishable, one from the other.

As there are many kinds and types of dances, each vital and invigorating for the particular moment or occasion, so it is with discipleship. There are times when our fear dissolves in the strong, driving wind that unseats us and allows the fiery tongue of faith to warm our frightened hearts in a passionate tango of life. At those moments, filled with God's holy spirit of love, light, and truth, we can express ourselves in ways previously foreign to us. Boldly prompted, we proclaim the marvels God has accomplished—no matter what it might cost, no matter the confused amazement it might bring.

At other moments, we remain locked behind the closed doors of our fear. No step is taken. No dancing can be done.

It is then that we come closest to comprehending the fact that God dwells in love, not fear. It is then that we begin to realize that "no one can say 'Jesus is Lord' except by the Holy Spirit" (1 Cor 12:3). God's spirit, though present in our fearfulness, is rendered powerless while terror holds reign. When fear is lord, Jesus is not!

The good news that emerged in the Pentecost event—and resurfaces with each inspirited dance of discipleship—is that Jesus will not let closed doors bar his entry into our lives. Even if we hang up our dancing shoes and lock the doors of the place where we are—whatever place that might be—Jesus comes to us while we are there. If we are frozen in positions of status or prestige, Jesus arrives. If we are held hostage by the need to be recognized and honored, Jesus appears. If we are hiding for fear of reprisal, isolation, or alienation, Jesus is there.

In the midst of all terror, there is Jesus—waiting to dance with us!

Our God comes to us where we are, stands before us so that we can clearly see that divine presence, and offers us the key to unlock the doors we had so carefully shut. "Peace be with you," says Christ, showing us pierced hands and side. These marks of his humanity are proof that he, too, was once afraid. He, too, was tempted not to be the Lord of the Dance. Peace—the shalom of wholeness and holiness—is ours while we keep our eyes sighted on our Messiah God.

It is not, however, a static peace of tranquility where all is well and remains so. It is the dynamic calm that lies serene under the storm, the quiet that pervades noise, the ease that prevents dis-ease. The peace of Christ is not solely a handshake of welcome. It is a soul-shaking introduction. We are being called into inspirational service—commissioned by a forgiving God into forgiveness. The peace of Christ breathes into us a loving spirit that impels us from fear to faith, bondage to freedom, death to life. It also empowers us to manifest that same spirit wherever we go.

Each of us is given a different route to travel in life, but the same Way to go. We are individually and uniquely called, but have the same mission. Our cups of life differ, but we drink of the same Spirit. "The body is one and has many members, and all the members of the body, though many, are one body, so it is with Christ" (1 Cor 12:12).

Our Pentecost is experienced in a multitude of ways, across myriad ages, in strange places, among those who are foreign to us as well as familiar. We are the Christ who comes and stands before those who are locked in their fears. We are God's conduits of inspired and inspiring love, inviting all to the shalom of divinity. We bear the awesome responsibility of forgiving sins— and the awful reality that we may hold others in bondage to sinfulness. Our effectiveness is directly proportionate to our receptiveness to the divine spirit of loving. Our dance is a mutual partnership, the movement of companions, or it is nothing at all.

There is reason to be fearful. If one partner falls, the other is in jeopardy. If the leader's position is usurped, the dance lacks balance. Pentecost is a frighteningly real experience. Its immensity should set us on our pins and cause contemplative concern. It is good for us to be gathered in fear—the holy, healthy fear of being less than we truly are. It is good to feel the power and hear the noise of God's strong driving wind, the gust that mightily pushes us into service. It is beneficial to see that each of us is indeed inflamed with divinity and filled with the Holy Spirit. No one is unimportant in that marvelously spiraling dance of discipleship—the delightful movement of fearful faith.

For Reflection and Discussion

- Thinking of discipleship as a dance, how would you describe yourself? Are you one who enjoys the rhythmic motion of a tango that keeps you within controlled parameters? Do you fancy a quick two-step, going from one action to another? Are you more inclined toward the free movements of jitterbug and be-bop? How is each a shadow of the other? In what ways have you both "fearfully gathered" as the family of God and "faithfully scattered" God's word?

Prayer

So it is fearfully that we gather, praying as we can...
    O most blessed Light divine,
    Shine within these hearts of yours,
    And our inmost being fill!
    Where you are not, we have naught,
    Nothing good in deed or thought,
    Nothing free from taint or ill.
    Heal our wounds, our strength renew;
    On our dryness pour your dew;
    Wash the stains of guilt away.

And faithfully, we scatter, helping to...
    Bend the stubborn heart and will;
    Melt the frozen, warm the chill;
    Guide the steps that go astray.

Believing, even behind locked doors, that God will
    Give us virtue's sure reward;
    Give us your salvation, Lord;
    Give us joys that never end.
    Amen, Alleluia!

        — Adapted from the Pentecost sequence

Susannah's story

My name is Susannah and I was there. It is as if it happened yesterday, the memory is so vivid in my mind and heart. The streets were teeming with people—as always happened during important holiday periods in Jerusalem. But this time, the air was charged with an unusual electricity. There was an atmosphere of excitement, exhilaration, and fascination. This year the Passover lamb would bleed twice—once for a meal and again on a cross. You may wonder at my words, but I believe what I believe because I have seen and wept over all I had witnessed.

Let me start at the beginning.

I had heard stories about the Nazorean—stories of patience and kindness but also of courage and conviction. I listened to tales of miracles performed in ways unknown to the other wonder-workers whose healings often bordered on magic, and who managed to baffle and bewilder people more than help them. The Nazorean was different, and his difference set him apart in ways that aroused the curiosity of the powerful priests and leaders of our land. I gasped when I learned he had confronted the Pharisees and Sadducees. There was never a happy ending when anyone took that path!

But until recently, these were only rumors and tales that had rumbled in the marketplace and were carried into the countryside through the conversations of shepherds and fishermen. Most of us had never met the man or seen his works. I decided that I would go to the city to see for myself who this Jesus was.

Passover would be a good reason for me to travel to Jerusalem and find a way to meet him, even if I only stayed on the edge of the crowd. In fact, I preferred that spot. It would let me remain an anonymous observer. Then I could decide if I wanted to draw closer or get away completely.

So, I left my hillside village and joined the pilgrims on the long, dusty trip. For most of us this was the trip of a lifetime. We could scarcely know how true those words would ring—nor how much we would be transformed by all we would see and experience!

Upon arrival, I managed to slip away from the group and asked some city dwellers where I could find this Jesus. Imagine my surprise when I learned he had already been tried in a court of law, made to walk a torturous route to Gethsemane, and crucified as a criminal among criminals.

Crucified!

I had been told that some considered him to be the Messiah. Crucifixion was an abomination of the Law. How could the Anointed One be crucified? It didn't make sense. I had to find someone with more information, someone who knew him. I had to uncover the truth or be destined to live with a lie.

There was a cluster of women who were furtively gathered near a house just inside the city. I sensed more than knew that they were followers of Jesus, so I went to them and asked if I might join them since I was a pilgrim with no place to stay. They hesitated for a moment. I saw them exchange glances. These were dangerous times with hidden enemies ready to slay and slaughter any and all who were dissenters. Silently, they nodded their heads, agreed to take a chance, and let me enter the house with them.

That was how I managed to be in the same room where Jesus' followers were praying. "What harm would come if I added my voice to theirs?" I thought. I dared to begin praising God in their midst. It seemed as if we had been praying for only a few minutes when I heard the sound. At first I thought it came from outside the house, but then I realized it was erupting from each of us. Each person had been carried on the wings of prayer so that we were no longer mumbling but were involuntarily shouting! We were no longer simply saying words. We had become the prayer and it was escaping us, filling the room with the roar of thunder.

Amazed, I opened my eyes ever wider as I gazed at each person individually. Surely I was mistaken. First I closed then reopened my eyes, to be certain of what I saw. They were glowing—faces bright with light; eyes sparkling with enthusiasm. It was as if they were on fire.

As I gazed around me, I was terrified. This was more than I could manage, more than I could imagine, explain, or understand. Then I became quiet, watching and listening. I let the love that filled the room envelop me. I felt comforted and accepted as one of the family. Relaxed, I returned to my praying. It was then that I heard the message of God.

Yes, you are hearing me rightly. It was God speaking to me in the words of these brothers and sisters. "Peace be with you. Receive the Holy Spirit." Clearly, I heard the command. But I knew it was given as a gift of love—not a demand of law.

I cried.

My tears were a mixture of joy and relief; compassion and release; wonder and love. I cried with the knowledge that I was loved by God. No more fears and terrors. No more confusion and criticism, only love. I was totally changed. And not just I. Every one of us became a new creation.

The room suddenly seemed too small. We could not be contained in it. What had happened to us could not remain our private gift. It had to be shared with all the earth. Fearing no one and nothing, we burst into the street—all of us speaking at the same time. All of us began giving the same message with wild abandon and wonderful awe: Jesus is Lord! Jesus is Lord! Jesus is Lord! We could not stop ourselves from speaking out.

A church was being born!

To this very day, I remain amazed at the sights and sounds and miracles I experienced so long ago. All I can say to you now—all I can give to you now—is my own constant prayer:

> Bless the Lord, O my soul! O Lord, my God, you are great indeed! How manifold are your works, O Lord! The earth is full of your creatures. When you send forth your spirit, they are created, and you renew the face of the earth. May the glory of God endure forever; may the Lord be glad in his works.

Oh, and I almost forgot what I came here to say to you: "Happy Birth-ing Day, dear church!"

For Reflection and Discussion

- Thinking of discipleship as a dance, how would you describe yourself? Are you one who enjoys the rhythmic motion of a tango that keeps you within controlled parameters? Do you fancy a quick two-step, going from one action to another? Are you more inclined toward the free movements of jitterbug and be-bop? How is each a shadow of the other? In what ways have you both "fearfully gathered" as the family of God and "faithfully scattered" God's word?

Prayer

Lord Jesus, I am honored to have you make my spirit your dwelling place. Help me to appreciate your delight in me. May my actions toward my neighbors always mirror your love.

— From *All Will Be Well*, based on the spirituality of Julian of Norwich

TRINITY SUNDAY

EXODUS 34:4–9; 2 CORINTHIANS 13:11–13; JOHN 3:16–18

Listening for God

My husband frequently says that most people spend most of their time looking for God and forget to listen for God. Yet psychologists continually remind us that learning and retention are more effective when we engage all our senses. If we applied that logic to our quest for God, listening for God would enhance looking for God—and vice versa.

When Moses climbed Mount Sinai early in the morning, he was doing so because he had listened for God and thus was made aware of God's command. His attentiveness did not end with his hearing the one message. It continued throughout the entire day and, indeed, his whole lifetime. Through clouds of doubt and despair, in fiery clarity and conviction, by light and in darkness, Moses listened for God. And God responded with the most intimate of communications. God's name was proclaimed. God's preeminence was announced. "The Lord, the Lord, a God merciful and gracious, slow to anger, and abounding in steadfast love and faithfulness" (Ex 34:6).

Often we look for God in all the wrong places and find a divinity too small to be true, too tiny to be authentic. At times we may listen to God, yet attend only to the sound of our own voices. Perhaps we hear those with whom we agree or who assent to our ideas of divinity, and pay no mind to dissenters. Worse yet, those with alternate understandings of God may be excluded from our presence or labeled demonic.

To listen for God is to intensify awareness that God speaks always and in all ways. To listen for God is to discover that God is triune. It is to comprehend that this trinitarian God speaks only love.

Universally and creatively, God loves, in order to nurture and sustain. This God, slow to anger, rich in kindness and fidelity, is not discouraged or dismayed by our wickedness or sinfulness. In the midst of the muck and mire in which we seem to entrench ourselves, there is God waiting to receive us as people who belong in divine embrace.

Why do we fight against believing this truth? Why would we rather a God we fear than one who loves unconditionally? Can it be that it is easier to comprehend and commit to a God who is made in our image and likeness than it is to follow one who has given us divinity and taken on our humanity to prove it?

I would suspect that is the case. We would rather serve a trinity of condemnation, strict judgment, and unrelenting punishment. Made in that image and likeness, inhumanity would be raised to great heights. No one need mend their ways. Discouragement would be virtue and encouragement denied. Harmony and peace would step aside to make room for chaos and fear. Holy kisses of shalom would become Judas touches that mock and mark for crucifixion.

In that deafening tumult of such an existence, listening for God is the task of the relentlessly restless ones who refuse to believe in a tiny trinity and will not surrender to impossibility. Like Moses in the pre-dawn dimness of Sinai's cloud or Nicodemus under cover of nocturnal darkness, those drawn to love by the limitlessly loving God listen for God in every event of their lives. God is heard in the signs and wonders performed before our very eyes, if only we will look and see inside the experiences. Where there is good, there is God. Where there is life and love and truth and justice, there is God. Where nurturing happens, creation is given room, and inspiration is appreciated, there is God. To listen for God is to become a God's conspirator. It is to inhale divinity—so that we might exhale the breath of God.

The words of Jesus to Nicodemus are spoken today to us. All life is summed up in one grand Yes! "For God so loved the world that he gave his only Son, so that everyone who believes in him may not perish but may have eternal life. Indeed, God did not send the Son into the world to condemn the world, but in order that the world might be saved through him" (Jn 3:16–17).

We are to listen for that God, the God whose only desire is to love us. We are to listen for the kind of loving God who would give all for one reason alone—that we might have eternal life. Listen for the God who does not condemn but wishes to save us from ourselves, to redeem us from the inhumanity we have labeled divine and the deity we have diminished to vengeance.

To listen for God and reveal love is to avoid condemnation. We avoid condemning as well as being condemned. Closed hearts are gracefully and gratefully opened to salvific truth. Eyes can now see God working in the world through flawed but faithful human beings. Slowly but surely, each of us begins to reflect the image of God who is merciful and gracious, slow to anger and rich in kindness and fidelity. Our stiff necks flex and stretch, allowing us to turn to see all the goodness that surrounds us. Cynicism collapses into charity; negativity is unnerved by nurture, and God is given room to be believed and believable.

To listen for God in the noisiness of discouragement is to be empowered to encourage. To listen for God in the turmoil of disharmony is to know peace and share peacefulness. To listen for God in the greetings of all God's holy ones is to understand community and share the eucharist that is Emmanuel. To listen for God is to be transformed by the grace of the Lord Jesus Christ, to be transfixed by the love of God, and to be transfigured by the companionship of the Holy Spirit.

To listen for God is to know, once and for all, that God is always with all of us. Not to believe the wonder of that love is to be condemned forever to live in the darkness of an inhumane, unholy desperation.

Why not listen for God and let Love come into our lives?

For Reflection and Discussion

- In what specific and deliberate ways have you been God's conspirator, inhaling divinity so that you might exhale God's breath and give life to a dying world? State recent incidents or occurrences where you have been listening for God in your family, friends, coworkers, and church members.

Prayer

Dear God, I have spent so much time listening to your voice in formal prayers and spiritual reading that I have forgotten how to listen for it in the ordinariness of my everyday life. Solomon asked for an understanding heart and was given one. I now ask to learn ways to listen for your voice in all the people I meet, especially those to whom I have often given a deaf ear. Let me listen for you in any criticism I receive, in opinions that differ from my own. Let me listen for you in little children as well as wise adults. Let me know that you are my God and I belong to you. Amen.

Heavenly bread, earthly food

Just as I sat down at the computer to reflect upon the relevance of the feast of Corpus Christi to today's world, the doorbell rang. Annoyed at the interruption, I roused myself to respond.

There in the doorway stood a young man and a little boy whom he introduced as his son. With a huge smile on his face, the gentleman quickly exchanged pleasantries and then launched into the reason for his presence. "I'd just like to talk with you about Jesus," he said. Inwardly, I groaned and thought, "Here we go. All I need right now is a visit with a Jehovah's Witness who won't take no for an answer." Adding to my upset was the fact that his son accompanied him. How could I dismiss the adult without giving poor example to the child? In answer to my unspoken question, I listened to his presentation with overt patience despite covert exasperation.

Surely this man believed that God was directing his journey and guiding his path through the desert. He and his son, quite literally, were making their way through parched land. They were ringing the doorbells of homes filled with the aridity of people who were busy about many things—even prayerful reflection—and did not wish to be disturbed. With patience tested and determination tried, he walked on, thirsting to share his understanding and experience of divinity, hungering to feed others with God's word, a food he believed still remained unknown to them, he moved from door to door. This man held the comfort and confidence that the God who brought him to his unique desert experience would remain there with him, as he made his pilgrimage out of slavery into freedom.

Like a host held high above the altar of consecration, he lifted his tract for me to see. Gustily he quoted from it, his words as sanctifying as any spoken in church. Whether or nor I agreed with his thesis, it was evident that his whole being vibrated with certitude that "one does not live by bread alone, but by every word that comes from the mouth of the Lord" (Deut 8:3). For him, heavenly bread was truly earthly food.

Our conversation ended abruptly when it became evident that I was not acquiescing to his statements or offering further opportunity for "conversion." He left my porch with my well wishes ringing in his ears. The door to my house closed and the two witnesses proceeded down the driveway to the road ahead.

And God walked with him and his son, while I marched resolutely to my computer.

As if for the first time, my own journey commenced. It was my turn to enter the hunger and thirst sated only by recognizing, receiving, remembering, and re-membering the body and blood of Christ. It was my time to walk, solemnly but smiling, into the aridity of faith without sight and hope held with radical optimism. When doors are slammed in my face—literally and figuratively—I will know something of broken bodies given to be living bread. When I, too, am eager to slake the thirst I sense in people who are not even cognizant that they are spiritually dehydrated, I shall taste the meaning of real drink.

Like Jesus, the Christ, who summons us to a new entry into life, so must I be a means of transfusing life into lifelessness. As he gave his body that we might be embodied in grace, so must I graciously offer my hopefulness to discouraged ones and my vitality to those who are listless. My life—and yours—must be spent in thanksgiving and forgiving, if we are to be witnesses of God's presence in an apparently godless world.

Eucharist must be more than a sacrament celebrated and received by a select few in special places at ordered times. The body and blood, soul and divinity we proclaim and announce has to be realized in the body and blood, soul and divinity we are to a world steeped in fleshiness but without body, one spilling over with gore but lacking grace, infused with specters but denied soul, one seeking superficiality instead of sanctity.

The Body and Blood of Christ feeds us all as we travel in the way of godliness. The Body and Blood of Christ nurtures us with the unity found of one loaf. If I were to be witness to the smiling duo who arrived at my doorstep, tracts in hand, it would be to leave them wondering about the possibility that we are all eating of the same loaf. We are all feeding on the same flesh and drinking of the same blood—whether we know it or not.

Our differences have taken heavenly bread and broken it into unrecognizable pieces. However, it has not changed in substance. God is no less God because we cannot agree that the same divinity infuses all of us equally. Our "religious" quarrels do not render God impotent. They diminish our effectiveness as the people of God, reducing our credibility to incredulity.

When we quarrel among ourselves we mimic the Jews questioning Jesus,

"How can he give us his flesh to eat?" We are more interested in the mechanics of the promise than the commitment itself. There is a sense that humans know intuitively that to partake of Christ…to eat and drink of the Christian life…is to be consumed by God, eternally. It is a priceless, but costly, resurrection that scares us as well as sanctifies.

We all love receiving heavenly bread. Our frightful faith is that we are commissioned to become what we eat. Heavenly bread is given and received as earthly food. And we are to be both recipients and donors. Partaking of Christ, we are now the body and blood of Christ given for all as real food and real drink. Those who feed on us feed on Christ. So nurtured, all will have life—to the full and forever.

For Reflection and Discussion

- In what parched lands have you walked, thirsting to share your understanding and experience of God? Who did you meet along that way? How did the experience affect you and them?

Prayer

Jesus my Savior, friend, companion and Lord, you have given us your very being as food for our journey. How great a gift; how often we fail to realize its worth! Come now into my heart, nurture my spirit, enkindle in me a deep appreciation of the nourishment you offer and the nurture I must give. Help me embody your presence to all who hunger and thirst. Lead me to them as you lead me home to you. Gratefully I ask, faithfully I believe that you are in me and I in you. Amen.

Ordinary
Time

Second Sunday in Ordinary Time

Isaiah 49:5–6; 1 Corinthians 1:1–3; John 1:29–34

As good as it gets

Serving often appears to be such a thankless task—perceived as a mundane, if not demeaning, duty. Servant: the word evokes images of wealthy aristocrats demanding unending labor and devotion from impoverished peons. It is a word that lives in a world of opposites: have vs. have not; powerful vs. powerless; superiors vs. inferiors. Yet, the Scriptures report this message of the Lord: "You are my servant, Israel, in whom I will be glorified" (Is 49:3).

Can it be that God is requiring an obeisance that destroys our personal uniqueness? Are we being asked to submit individuality to the anonymity of silent servanthood? Is that the only pathway for God's glory to be evidenced? Something deep inside of me recoils at the thought. I question the logic that implies a need for absence in order that presence be known. I ask myself how it is possible to image God by disappearing, imaging nothing at all.

Perhaps our notions of service are at the core of the problem. Isaiah hints at a resolution. "It is too light a thing that you should be my servant," says God. We cannot retain tiny definitions of servanthood. Instead, we must push the envelope, break open the boundaries, see that serving encompasses all walks of life and takes many shapes. When service consciously becomes ministry everything changes. Dreaded duty gives way to dedicated discipleship.

Recently, I gave myself an afternoon treat and spent a couple of hours watching the movie *As Good As It Gets*. Within the space of a few frames, I became engrossed in the weird antics of Melvin Udall. It was not much longer before his obsessive compulsive behavior echoed some of my own personal "craziness." Each of us harbors a variety of oddities that we hold close in our individual comfort zones. While we retain saner thoughts in our heads, we still bumble along in those places where, for now, this is as good as it gets. At the same time, we sense the untruth of such limitation. What we need is exactly what Melvin received: service beyond the call of duty.

Melvin got what he required in the person of a waitress named Carol. She had her own problems and could easily have dismissed him as just one more burden. Instead, she recognized dis-ease and sought to bring ease. She comforted and consoled through her acceptance. It was not that Carol was unaware of Melvin's different behavior. It was that she saw beyond it. She saw the person who sustained hurt much more than he lashed out in hatred. When all others fled to escape contact with him, Carol waited on him, treating him as she would any other patron.

We need someone to wait on us, to wait for us, to stoop toward us and hear our cry. As the waitress Carol permitted Melvin to be who he was yet refused to allow him to remain stuck in that mud, so do we crave a similarly perceptive servant-minister.

The movie continued through many twists and turns. But the theme of serving and waiting, waiting and serving knit both story and characters together. Little by little, each became servant for the other—sometimes willingly and other times by force. Lack of positive motivation was not a deterrent. It became grounds for conversion. Annoyances slowly turned into opportunities for affection. What had been hated and treated with caustic comment, gradually was the object of concern. No one was presented as perfect. Nor was anyone totally flawed. The premise was that all are redeemable when each becomes servant of the other.

Each of us is gifted with divine glory. Our presence is meant to be "a light to the nations, that my salvation may reach to the end of the earth" (Is 49:6). However, the dust and grime of day-to-day existence dulls the lamp, reducing its capacity and dimming its power. Someone has to clear away the grit so that our brilliance will return. Someone has to put up with all the junk we dish out. Someone has to serve us with unstinting devotion.

Through thick and thin, good times and bad, the people of God catch sight of Jesus coming toward us. It matters not that we do not readily recognize him. What is important is that we realize our inability; we are aware of our clouded sight and carry on! Our mission is always to be sharpening our focus. We are to be on the lookout for the Spirit of God, noticing where that spirit descends and comes to rest. We are servant-ministers who point the way to holiness.

It is not so difficult to do, especially if the awareness begins at the level of ordinary things done by ordinary people. I know that I see God's spirit in my next door neighbors. They are elderly folks who are bearing the ravages of time. Their dependency on hearing aids, walking aids, and oxygen is displaced as their faces light up with the joy of having a new puppy come into their home. Look there, I tell myself, and recognize God.

I hear my grandchildren squeal with delight when we visit. Look there and see the God who takes joy in being with us. I visit my mother to celebrate her eighty-ninth birthday and notice wrinkles turn into wreathed smiles. Look, there is the God who crinkles with pleasure that we have come to call. The phone rings, a friend asks me to go shopping with her or to the movies. Look, there is the God who never stops inviting us to venture out. I witness a young mother who comes unfailingly to church week after week with her wheel-chair-bound son. I hear the soulful sounds emerge from his damaged nervous system. Look, there is the God who cared enough to wrap divinity in flawed flesh.

Look here, look there, look everywhere—and wait. Wait for the Lord who stoops towards us, hears our cry, and puts a new song into our mouths. Wait to be, become, and empower servant-ministers through whom shines the glory of God.

It's as good as it gets!

For Reflection and Discussion

• When have you experienced the God who stoops towards us, hears our cry, and puts a new song into our mouths? Who has helped you to venture out and be surprised by divinity? Describe the times when you have realized an inability or became aware of your clouded sight, and yet carried on in faith and faithfulness.

Prayer

Dear God, sometimes I feel too little to be anything more than a slave to my own inadequacy. I live in the shadows of your presence and fear coming into the light. Yet I believe that you are with me always. I trust that you have anointed me with your holy Spirit. I want to be your servant. I want to be one who will be a light to the nations of my own tiny world. I want to bring back to you all who have strayed, including myself. Do not let my fear become a fatal obstacle. Implant in me a spirit of radical trust and continue to impel me in the ways of truth and justice. I ask this in the name of my companion, savior, and brother, Jesus the Christ. Amen.

THIRD SUNDAY IN ORDINARY TIME

ISAIAH 8:23–9:3; 1 CORINTHIANS 1:10-13, 17; MATTHEW 4:12-23

A divided Christ is a meaningless cross

Each year, many Christians observe a week of prayer for Christian unity. It would seem that the power of prayer, individual and collective, would have long since achieved its goal and all would be one in Christ. Yet the division remains. Many times the golden jubilee door has been opened, then closed on the proverbial twelve months of reprieve. Nothing has changed.

It would seem that Christianity has stalemated at the juncture found in Paul's letter to the Corinthians. We who would follow the Christ as one body have instead divided that body into parts. Each has become a faction quarreling for power and loyalty. Each strives to crucify the other on the wood of denominational rules. Worse yet there is friction within each group.

We divide Christ into parts—and render the cross void of meaning!

This is a harsh indictment of Christians and a severe portrait of a pushing/tugging/bickering people. Sad to say, it is also a true one. We are a people living in darkness who refuse the great light of love that continues to gleam in our midst. We have chosen a cross that has not been resurrected and seem to persist in rejecting unity in favor of uniformity. We seek to enslave the Christ who lived and died that we might be free to share liberty and justice with all—instead of embracing him in each other.

The problem is pervasive. It is not limited to one denomination or another but snakes insidiously into each and all. Pastors who have total power inflict their sole judgment and singular decisions on the entire parish while parishioners sit submissively in pews. Congregations with similar potency hold their pastor hostage to individual whims and wishes, taunting him or her with refusal of tithes. The "build a new church" people fight the "stay where we are" folks—and vice versa.

One theology battles another. Moderates berate liberals. Charismatics wave arms in praise and call it the only prayer there is. Social activists declare the primacy of their cause while restorationists decry change of any sort. Sin is categorized into levels of depravation—and sinners follow suit.

What is wrong with this picture? It seems, at first blush, to be a problem of such dimension that no resolution can be had. However, I suspect the answer is not quite so complicated. In fact, it is incredibly simple and found in two intertwining sentences: "Reform your lives," and "The kingdom of God is at hand."

Inseparable truths, they urge us to leave our former existence that was masked as reality and enter the real world. Depart from all labors that focus on egocentricity and come into the reign of theocentricity. Stop casting nets into a sea of darkness where might is right and quantity rules over quality. Abandon all activity that entraps and keeps us in repetitive motion. Stop racing through life like laboratory mice traveling in fatiguing movements that erode our being and infuse us with a sense of helpless futility. Peer through the cages of life and see that God's reign is here and now—immediately at hand, if only we will note its presence.

To form our lives differently is to recognize God's reign. To pay heed to God's rule is synonymous with the reformation of our lives. The two movements form a synchronized dance of divinity. In partnership, God leads and we follow. God directs and we decide. God calls and we respond.

Marching into truth, waltzing delightedly with justice, slow-dancing in the ballroom of peace, this magnificent interdependence provides the music and magic of a lifetime. There is no room for discordant notes, but there is room for disagreement and charitable confrontation. None are coerced into compliance. All are encouraged to sing in harmony. Audiences will be captivated by the sounds and silences, but never held captive by noisy dispute!

Gone is the need to be Numero Uno. That place is open for God. Instead of power plays and status seeking, there is compassion and creativity. Justice is optimal; judgment held in abeyance. The burdensome yoke of uniformity, the terrible weight of polarity, the horrible rod of righteousness have all been smashed by the God who loves all equally. What God has put asunder no one may now reunite!

To follow Christ is to journey into a place where healing replaces hating; faith ousts factions; light banishes darkness. It is a place and space where "they will look to the earth, but will see only distress and darkness, the gloom of anguish; and they will be thrust into thick darkness" (Isa 8:22). The only reunion there can be is the restoration of the Body of Christ into parts that work cooperatively though differently. The only cross to be borne is the one that Jesus carried—a tool that brought resurrection through crucifixion, life through death, salvation from slavery.

All the world aches for this reality. Too few are willing to walk the Way that leads to it. We want the end but reject the means to achieve it; we desire the gain and refute the pain. We seek to find light in the tunnel of life without ever entering the darkness of the unknown that will reveal it. So we make crosses of our own choosing and nail others to them, crucifying life and creating death. We defy God's unity and deny divinity by dividing Christ's body and rendering Christ's cross meaningless.

For those who choose to fish in the seas of humanity, toil in the vineyards of God's reign, walk the way of goodness, and see meaning in the cross, dividing the body of Christ is anathema. Working for unity, surfacing anonymous Christians everywhere, they cry for patience and labor for universality. Their prayer can be heard along the highways and byways God's people tread: Be stouthearted, and wait for the Lord who is the light, salvation, and refuge of life. Wait with the strength found in unity—the unity discovered in being of one mind and heart.

For Reflection and Discussion

- The gospel tells us that true discipleship involves leaving our nets behind. What nets are holding you back from your desire to follow Christ? Which one are you throwing into the sea of discipleship? Are you casting for what you see and like or for what you need for nourishment and nurturing? If there is any disunity or division in your faith family, what specific actions can you take to empower unity?

Prayer

Lord Jesus, your final prayer on earth was a plea that we might all be one as you are one with the Father in the Spirit of Love. Give us the sight and insight to recognize the areas in our life where there is disunity, discord, or division. Give us the courage, strength, and wisdom to reveal those areas and transform them. If anything is entrapping us, keeping us from both seeing and doing our mission as disciples, please remove the obstacles so that we might be ever more aware of our call and commission to follow your lead. In gratitude, we pray. Amen.

FOURTH SUNDAY IN ORDINARY TIME

ZEPHANIAH 2:3, 3:12–13; 1 CORINTHIANS 1:26–31; MATTHEW 5:1–12

Searching for God

Too many people want to sit out life complacently. Some of us argue that we are on the downside of life's hill, have already expended our energies, and are now entitled to retirement. Our aim is to do as little as possible, sliding lazily toward a demise we hope will come stealthily, while we sleep. Others are busily climbing that same hill, burdened with jobs, rearing children, stealing time to relax—time that is instead spent frenetically chasing fun. In neither case is there a sincere search. In both instances, escape is the motivation.

Yet if we are to become the spiritual persons God has called us to be, we must always be seekers. As Henri Nouwen wrote in the introduction to *Merton's Palace of Nowhere*, by James Finley,

> The spiritual life is to be earnestly pursued as though no spiritual life existed. This is the only safe and sane way to travel in the deep waters of the spirit….There is only one life, and that is God's life which he gives to us from moment to moment, drawing us to himself with every holy breath we take. The quest for God is centered wholly upon God and not upon the various thoughts and feelings we may happen to have along the way.

We cannot escape the quest.

We are among those called to seek, search, probe, question, and rest in the magnitude of the God who "is the source of your life in Christ Jesus" (1 Cor 1:30). God asks that we opt for radical "be-ing" not surface "existing." This requires an openness to surprising possibilities—a "be-attitudinal" lifestyle!

Paul's message to the Corinthians rings true for us today. Not many of us are wise, as wisdom is humanly accounted; not many are influential; and surely not many are well-born. The reality is that "God chose what is foolish in the world to shame the wise; God chose what is weak in the world to shame the strong; God chose what is low and despised in the world, things that are not, to reduce to nothing things that are" (1 Cor 1:27–28).

No headhunter would eagerly accept us as clients. But God is not a headhunter foraying in the field of humanity to find the best and brightest for an upwardly mobile kingdom. God has chosen us in our absurdity, calling us to boast only in the Lord. Our weakness thus shames the strong. Our absurdity outwits the wise. Our humility challenges the high-born. The power people of the world are puzzled by the purity of our purpose. Their "happiness" is assaulted by the potency of our joy in the midst of apparent impoverishment

What we know or possess means little in the reign of God. All that matters is that we continue to imitate Christ as Christ images the Father—especially via his incarnation of the message of Isaiah 61. That topsy-turvy world, the reign of God, is uniquely expressed in the Matthean beatitudes. Happiness is harbored in sorrow and pain. It is not an easy message gliding smoothly from saccharine platitudes. It is the story told by those who seek and find the God who was always there.

I once received a note from a friend that hit my heart. She wrote: "Living for your faith is more painful than dying for it. Don't give up." I read and reread those words, letting them soak into the very fiber of my being. There is no modifier to soften the wisdom contained there—just the plain, simple statement of ongoing process, intense probing, and responsive pain. Her words are matter of fact, though not without compassionate understanding. Being a beatitude Christian is living for one's faith—and it is more painful than dying for it. It is a martyrdom of pulsating witness that brings vitality where morbidity had once held reign.

To die for faith may be a blaze of glory. To live for it is to be a burning ember that glows long after the blaze has disappeared.

As burning embers, we serve to re-ignite banked or forgotten fires. We help all whose flame of love has been lost in a misguidedly rigid observation of the law. Ignoring justice and missing humility, they wander aimlessly and unhappily, knowing that there is a vacuum in their life. Unaware of its cause, they are unable to fill it. Having hampered their capacity to seek, finding and possessing true blessedness eludes them. Life becomes a sad illusion.

All that we are not rankles. Poverty, sorrow, lowliness, hunger and thirst for holiness, single-heartedness, peacemaking, persecution, insults, and slander are all perceived as punishments from a God who delights in our misery. The wonder of quest is replaced by whining questioning, "Why me?" Life's focus makes a massive turn from other to self. Once that happens, there is a serious risk of forgetting our dependency on God and becoming self-righteously complacent, pleased with ourselves.

Given the choice, I daresay most of us would opt for having worldly wisdom, influence, strength, being well-born and well-liked. The problem lies not in what we like but in how it affects our ability, motivation, and will to seek the Lord who loves us in our lowliness: "God does not come into our world with the toughness of an omnipotent thug, to sort everything and everybody out. He himself has chosen the way of weakness. There is something about God which is better expressed in weakness than in strength, in foolishness than in wisdom, in poverty than in richness" (*The Beatitudes: Soundings in Christian Traditions*, Simon Tugwell, OP).

It is this "something about God" that we seek to imitate as people of the Beatitudes. Our goal is not poverty, sorrow, hunger, thirst, persecution, or slander. We would be masochists in that case. Our goal is God *found* in poverty, sorrow, justice, persecution, and slander. Our attitude is one of "be-ing," of finding good where evil appears, grace where there seems only to be greed.

We can only attain our goal, touch our God, as seekers, one step at a time, searching as we journey into mystery, paradox, and life.

For Reflection and Discussion

• Discuss the various ways in which you have or may now begin to search for God in your daily life. How can you find happiness in sorrow and pain? What examples can you give, from your own life or that of others, that demonstrate the pain that is experienced in living for your faith? How did/does that pain serve as a pointer or pathway in the search for God? When have you been a blaze of glory? A burning ember?

Prayer

O, My God
I offer you this day,
All that I might think or do or say;
Uniting it with what was done
By Jesus Christ your only Son.
Take my body, Jesus,
Eyes and ears and tongue.
Never let me, Jesus,
Help to do you wrong.
Take my heart and fill it
Full of love for you.
All I have I give you.
Give yourself to me. Amen.

Rising light dispels the gloom of night

I have always been repelled by statements that are followed by commands. I feel manipulated and threatened by them. Usually the result is that I retreat into angry silence. I resent being told what to do, especially when the telling has been sweetened with a compliment, such as "You do it so well that...." It seems less than honest to me. and is not a good feeling. Yet I am now hearing my God saying and doing just that!

"You are the salt of the earth. You are the light of the world," God tells me. But, what if salt goes flat? What if the light is hidden? What if you are not what I have made you to be? Well, then, you are good for nothing!

What kind of God would say that to me? Who would offer compliments and then refute them if they are not heard and heeded? Despite my initial reaction of anger and dismay, I must admit that this is a God of radical honesty—a God who tells it like it is and pulls no punches in the process. I am too important to God to be dismissed with pious platitudes or saccharine sanctity. I am worth more than mediocrity. I belong to a God who asks of me all that I already am—and therefore can be. This is my kind of God, though not always one I consider to be a kind God! This is the God in whose image I have been made and whose power courses through me.

One of my daughters called recently to tell me that she feels intimidated by coworkers whose intelligence surpasses hers, whose glibness of tongue is matched with her stammering phrases. She is nearly in tears with the pain of feeling less than adequate, despite the fact that her resume includes presentations that have received rave reviews. In here mind, her "flaws" now loom larger than her successes. Discouraged, she is in danger of falling into the heresy that she is good for nothing.

So I remind her that she is "salt" for the earth, that is, the world in which she lives and travels. If she allows intimidation to overpower her, her saltiness will indeed go flat. She will have allowed her self-esteem to be thrown out and her goodness will be for naught—and her intimidators will never have been given the opportunity to see life differently.

However, this does not have to happen. My voice rises with passion as I tell my daughter that her savory spirit, her light and love, are meant to be shared, not hidden. It is too easy—and at the same time, too difficult—to say that her sharing needs to be universal. I offer a suggestion: whittle down the "everyone list."

Start with those who are most in need. Instead of attempting to please people who find displeasure in all that she is and does, I advise her to share the bread of life with those who are truly hungry for it. Rather than sheltering herself from the slings and arrows that accompany true vitality, I propose that she give the home of her heart to those who are oppressed and homeless. Instead of covering her vulnerability with avoidance and denial, I ask that she clothe the naked needy with hope and courage. These remnant people, tattered and torn, are brothers and sisters. My daughter cannot turn her back on her own. Nor can we.

Fear of failure cannot seduce her into leaving in the lurch all of us who share the terrible beauty of being real in an unreal world Her pain is ours and ours is hers, the gift that saves us both!

Amazingly, the very fact that she continues to journey this earthly life in weakness and fear, and with much trepidation, is testimony to the fact she is living a message that has none of the persuasive force of "wise" argumentation—only the convincing power of the Spirit. As a consequence, our faith—the faith of all who walk with her—rests not on her wisdom, but on the power of God.

Another, equally wondrous, phenomenon occurs. Helping others helps my daughter. Hearing their call, her cry will be heeded. While removing oppression, her own burden will be lifted. False accusations and malicious speech will vanish in the heat of her truth. Healing others, she will be quickly healed.

Her rising light dispels the gloom of personal negativity and becomes dawn for her own darkness.

As I speak to her, the words reverberate in my own being. I am my daughter as much as she is me. There is in both of us—in all of us—an "I Am" that will not be hidden. We are the light of the world. We stand on a divine pedestal, heightened so that our brilliance may more forcefully brighten the shadows and banish fear. Gracious, merciful, just, unmoving, firm of heart and trusting in God, we bring enduring generosity to an impoverished humanity, a people that falsely gives credence to the murky spirits of fear, power, and self-centeredness.

What I tell my daughter, I hear myself. The "I Am" that I am is the salt of the earth. If I, if you, if we allow that salt to go flat, how can the flavor of grace be restored? Will we allow ourselves to be good for nothing when God's desire is that we be goodness for everything?

Ours is a God of radical honesty—a God who tells it like it is and pulls no punches in the process. I am too important to God to be dismissed with pious platitudes or saccharine sanctity. I am worth more than mediocrity. I belong to a God who asks of me all that I already am and therefore can be. This is my kind of God—though not always one I consider to be a kind God! This is the God in whose image I have been made and whose power courses through me.

This is the God whose rising light dispels the gloom and becomes dawn for our darkness.

For Reflection and Discussion

- When have you felt good for nothing? How did that feeling affect your sense of discipleship? In what ways can you change those feelings by thoughts? Through actions? How do you see yourself as too important to God to be dismissed with saccharine sanctity? Being worth more than mediocrity?

Prayer

Christ, as a light, illumine and guide me.
Christ, as a shield overshadow and cover me.
Christ, be under me; Christ, be over me.
Christ, be beside me, on the left and the right.
Christ, be before me, behind, about me.
Christ, the lowly and meek; Christ, the all powerful,
Be in the heart of each of whom I speak,
In the mouth of each who speaks to me,
In all who draw near me, or see me, or hear me. Amen.

—Attributed to St. Patrick

Sixth Sunday in Ordinary Time

Sirach 15:15–20; 1 Corinthians 2:6–10; Matthew 5:17–37

Scrutinizing the deep things of God

How often I have heard someone tell me to lighten up, cool my jets, chill out—or words to that effect! It seems that deep thinking is far less popular an activity than deep sea diving. Do religion, if you want, but don't be a fanatic about it. Any tendency to profound pondering is annoying, if not anathema!

Yet the Scriptures ask us to join in a Spirit-led venture, scrutinizing the deep things of God. There can be no lightening up or chilling out, no cooling of jets here. Instead, what is needed is heavy thinking that heats up the heart and is catalytic energy for intense contemplation. God wants us to examine divinity—to scrutinize its depth and surface its dynamism.

We have before us fire and water, life and death. Whichever we choose shall be given to us. That is God's divine promise—and our human selection!

I can still picture the Count in the movie *Chocolat*—a man who has substituted self-imposed penance for other-centered zestful living. Controlled and controlling, he quite literally held open the door to a narrowly defined and understood holiness—or slammed it shut in the face of those who did not meet his standards. For the Count, to scrutinize the deep things of God was to find only arrogant dismissal and angry denial of all who were different or saw things differently. To delight in change was to defy depth and select superficiality. It was also to court death.

Into this dance of death, on the wings of the North wind, came Vianne and her daughter Anouk, an inspirited duo whose colorful presence soon seduced an entire town with the innocent pleasure of being. The door to their chocolaterie was opened wide with the wisdom of God who sees all as good and understands human deeds. Their happiness, born in pain and borne with power, was infectious. Symbolized in chocolate choices laced with peppery potency, Vianne knew intuitively exactly what each townsperson needed in order to be truly alive. She gave free tastes of vivacity—samples of the wonders dormant within each of them, the possibilities they had long since buried under a heavy blanket of order for order's sake.

Her insistence on justice for all and her blatant refusal to participate in superficiality empowered cowering women and gave voice to silenced children. A mourning widow who had lost life when her husband died rediscovered vitality. A vagabond gypsy troupe found acceptance in their unacceptability. An embittered grandmother's hard facade was softened as her frigidly straitlaced daughter's demeanor gained gentle, genuine openness.

Each person in the village was touched in ways they alone knew by Vianne—the oddly different woman who scrutinized the deep things of God, walked in God's law, happily observing divine decrees with open eyes and compassionate heart. Wherever she went, she carried with her an "ark of the covenant" she had with her God. For Vianne, it was the urn bearing her mother's ashes. This was her amulet of choice, her reminder that "no eye has seen, nor ear heard, nor the human heart conceived, what God has prepared for those who love him" (1 Cor 2:9).

The ashes brought life to an otherwise fatal existence. They evoked scrutiny of things divinely creative where she might have been caught up in the superficiality of human rigidity. The ashes gave her encouragement in the face of deadening discouragement and hope in the sight of hopelessness. The strange vigor contained in that urn was enough to maintain Vianne's commitment to say yes when she meant yes and no when she meant no. The ashes of that urn became the mainstay, the law, that ruled Vianne's life and embraced all who feel under the spell of her sparkling vivaciousness.

One day the urn would not be enough. Vianne would have to decide again to scrutinize the deep things of God before she could relieve her restless running, no matter how much good that had wrought in all the places she had been. Even the urn would have to be broken in order to set free God's spirit. And it was broken—by the child she loved so dearly. Her own Anouk refused to run from the pain of superficiality. She wanted to remain in the town. She wanted to be herself in a place where control prevailed. Whether by chance or providence, her decision to pull away from Vianne's vehement stance also caused her to drop the urn which shattered and scattered its ashy contents.

It was a critical moment for mother and daughter—a crucial experience that bore life and death, fire and water. The breaking of the urn was not an abolishment of all that they had experienced in life. It was an opportunity for fulfillment. It was a time to give significance even to the most insignificant of episodes.

With the magic of movies, all happened in the blink of an eye. Anouk tried to gather the ashes, returning them and their bearers to life as it was. Vianne contemplated the dilemma, scrutinized it deeply, and flung the ashes to the wind which bore them beyond barriers and to far spaces.

Consciously or unconsciously, deliberately or not, mother and daughter had asked for discernment with each step they had taken. Every time they flaunted the letter of the law and sought its spirit, they grew in ability to observe God's will and keep it with all their hearts. Their growth seeded another's harvest.

So, also, will it go for us—and with us. We are the Viannes and Anouks of the world who counter the control of Counts seeking a rigid rule. Their rigor, in effect, abolishes the very law they attempt to protect and promote. Their refusal to scrutinize the deep things of God results in an mortal embrace of the superficial. Instead of dancing into life, there is a steadfast march into death. Instead of fire, there is only a watery existence that lacks luster. We are left aching for chocolate—and God.

For Reflection and Discussion

- How do you see the law of God being fulfilled in your life? In what ways can you go beyond the law to enter the kingdom of justice and mercy? State the ways in which you can scrutinize all matters, even the deep things of God.

Prayer

Happy are those who do not follow the advice of the wicked, or take the path that sinners tread, or sit in the seat of scoffers;

but their delight is in the law of the Lord, and on his law they meditate day and night.

They are like trees planted by streams of water, which yield their fruit in its season, and their leaves do not wither.

In all that they do, they prosper.

The wicked are not so, but are like chaff that the wind drives away.

Therefore the wicked will not stand in the judgment, nor sinners in the congregation of the righteous;

for the Lord watches over the way of the righteous, but the way of the wicked will perish.

—Psalm 1

The painful pleasure of being perfected

Teasingly, my husband has often confronted me with a statement delivered to the air surrounding us: "It must be wonderful to be perfect. One day, perhaps, I will be as perfect as you are." His sarcasm does not suffer from subtlety! With sword swiftness it cuts through to the heart of the matter, exposing the marrow of my need to be in control. As Scripture says, my husband catches me, the "wise one," in the throes of my craftiness.

When I point out his inadequacies, I laud my efforts. When he is found lacking, I am discovered as more than adequate. His failures are my successes. The speck on his washed dish makes my pot sparkle by comparison. His memory loss is my gain. His slowness demonstrates my speed. And the list goes on. That kind of perfection is more about doing things the way I think they should or must be done and less about learning new ways, new ideas, new concepts that might make me a better person.

The call of the gospel—for that matter, the cry of Leviticus—is about being perfected. Its command is "be holy, for I am holy" (Lev 11:44). That's it, in a nutshell. What we determine to be the content of this holiness, how we attain and maintain it, is a whole other story. It is the saga of a lifetime—and it begins with blessing the God who has made us icons of divinity.

So what is holiness? If I look to God as exemplar, my answer is both simple and profound. It is the pleasure and pain of being a whole person—someone who never forgets benefits and pardons all iniquities. It is a person who heals all ills and redeems others from possible destruction, crowning them, instead, with kindness and compassion. Holy ones are those who are merciful and gracious, slow to anger, and abounding in kindness. They do not requite according to crimes but put transgressions far from those who commit them. Holy people know, honor, and respect the fact that they abide in the Spirit of God—and God abides in them.

An aura surrounds holy people that both attracts and repels. We like to be with them as much as we fear their presence. Their transparency brings light to our opaqueness; their openness gives pause to our parsimoniousness. Holy ones command a certain process of being perfected because they themselves are immersed in it. Being perfected is their way of life, their mode of existence. They are ready to be transformed, changed—for the better—at all times and with all people. An excitement for God, a profound and serious enthusiasm, marks their way. It sparks in them a vitality that is meant to be shared for the invigoration of the world.

Holy people are different. Their power is fueled with powerlessness and a hunger for the kind of justice that is indiscriminately universal. More than giving the shirt off their back, they will hand over their coat as well. Less is not more in their book—at least not when it comes to giving. Holiness is nothing if it is not replete with generosity.

I listened to the story of a divorced woman who deliberately set out to maintain a friendship with her ex-husband although their separation could easily have been ugly, hateful, and hurtfully divisive. She spoke of praying long and hard before beginning the struggle toward amicability. At first, it was done pragmatically. Her labor was centered on avoiding long battles that would set family members against each other. Soon, however, it began to dawn on her that she was being changed. What could have been a lifetime of lonely bitterness became an experience of love. She was being perfected—and holy is her name.

I know two sisters who find it more than difficult to deal with their vastly different temperaments. They want to be friends as well as relatives but cannot seem to unveil a common ground. Each believes that the other is pressing her into service for two miles and is willing only to go the one—if that! Each sees the other as begging for more than is deserved. They want an eye for an eye, a tooth for a tooth. Yet, having tried to extract that kind of justice, they remain wanting more—and getting less.

One cries out, "Why is it always me who has to take the initiative and make the first move?" The other stays silently distant with identical words taking harbor in the depth of her spirit. Each awaits the perfection of the other without approaching their own need to be perfected. Their ache, a soul-soreness, is painful to watch and hurts the heart—theirs and mine alike.

I can say much to each one or say little. It will not really matter until each one is ready to hear—really hear—the cry of Scripture: "You shall be holy, for I the Lord your God am holy" (Lev 19:1).

No one can make us hear and respond to those words. Only we ourselves can finally come to the conclusion that nothing else really works. No retribution, no vengeance, no grudge bearing, no punishment, no persecution of our persecutors can match the wholesome holiness that is ours when we stop seeking perfection and start searching for ways to be perfected.

Though it is admittedly not an easy task, it is only when we actively enter into the process of becoming people who love that we taste the painful pleasure of being perfected. Hurts will still be ours, but they will not destroy us. Pain will continue to plague our steps, but it will not take our breath away. Death-dealing darkness will no longer be a part of living. In its stead, there will only be the bright promise born in the heart of holiness.

Be holy and know that all things are ours. And we are Christ's. And Christ is God's. That is the pleasure that surmounts the pain of being perfected.

For Reflection and Discussion

- How can you begin and continue to be holy as God is holy? Give examples of ways in which you can intensify the process of being and becoming a person who loves. What steps can you take to empower a loving lifestyle in your family and in the family of God?

Prayer

Holy God we praise your name.
Lord of all we bow before you.
All on earth your scepter claim.
All in heaven above adore you;
Infinite your vast domain.
Everlasting is your name. Amen.

—*Te Deum Laudamus*

EIGHTH SUNDAY IN ORDINARY TIME

ISAIAH 49:14–15; 1 CORINTHIANS 4:1–5; MATTHEW 6:24–34

Let tomorrow take care of itself

I never cease to be amazed that Scripture is simultaneously consoling and challenging. Today's gospel passage is a magnificent example. Jesus reminds us that we cannot serve two masters. We will either "hate the one and love the other, or be devoted to the one and despise the other. You cannot serve God and wealth. Therefore I tell you, do not worry about your life, what you will eat or what you will drink, or about your body, what you will wear" (Mt 6:24–25). There is nothing in this world I need to worry about. God will take care of everything. At the same time, I know that I will never reach that level of consolation until and unless I enter the challenge that is involved in not worrying!

The task, for me, is often monumental. I give everything to God, and take it back before the words have left my mouth. I travel back and forth in my rocking chair of worry, using energy to go nowhere. It is as if the motion itself will be my salvation. Despite the futility of the action, I seem unable to resist it. I want to be attentive to both masters. I cannot let go of anxiety nor can I give faith the freedom to move and breathe as God wills. It is not that I do not believe so much as it is that I am afraid to make so radical a commitment. I want to hedge my bets, keep an ace up my sleeve, and have an array of responses to any "what if" that may emerge along the way. Truth be told, I want to be in total control of my life—and the lives of others, as well.

Yet in my heart of hearts, I know that it is only in God that my soul is at rest. Only from God comes my salvation. God alone is my rock and my salvation, my stronghold. My deepest hope abides solely in God.

And my seesaw of faith and fear continues to rise and fall.

Perhaps the most severe test of discipleship is its radical call to choose between masters. Are we to be mastered, owned, and led by fear or by faith? Which will we follow? By which will we be disciplined?

The questions may roll easily from mind and mouth but the answers come more slowly and with greater hesitation. Life in the South annually impels me into a greater understanding of the angst that underlies my faith response. When hurricane season strikes, I wax and wane before the tides of faith and fear. Clear visions of total loss come tumbling into my imagination. Just as acute is the accompanying question, "Am I ready to lose everything I own?" Instantaneously, I shout "No!" So, I begin my summertime psalter of intercession. "Please God send the hurricanes into the sea. Let them not come our way nor the way of any other humans. Please."

The begging, I hope and pray, does not belie my faith nor undermine my faithfulness. It is the cry of one who believes that life is more important than food and the body more valuable than clothes. It is also the plea of one finds it difficult to learn lessons from the way wildflowers grow and birds of the sky live because I am neither.

I am human. I have all the frailty that resides in humanity, and all the hope that keeps us going. I do not worry over what I am to eat or drink or wear but I am less able to resist being anxious over the loss of health or sight or hearing or ability to think or speak. Running after material goods is not a kind of unbelief; uneasiness with confrontation, challenge, and committed criticism is. I do not want to believe that I have a prophetic mission to pursue and promote. I do not want to give complete credence and commitment to the reality that God knows all that I need. It is a scary way to live.

Instead of tending solely to this moment, this day, this task, I would much rather worry incessantly about all that might occur tomorrow. That kind of concern has an insidious effect on the psyche. It prevents my doing anything creative today! It keeps me from encountering the adventure, surprise, vitality, and sacredness of the present moment, a time often noted as the eighth sacrament. Fear of tomorrow destroys faith in today. An amazing God disappears from sight in the maze of agitation.

So, I come full circle. The choice cannot be avoided without severe deprivation to my truest self. I am the one who suffers most when I do not choose. True for me, it is also a human verity. None of us can escape the need to choose our master. We must select the one whom we will serve or flounder and be lost in indecisiveness. We must trust that Isaiah confronted us with God's truth when he both asked a question and answered it. "Can a woman forget her nursing child, or show no compassion for the child of her womb? Even these may forget, yet I will not forget you" (Is 49:15).

We can take the chance of commitment because God has already risked radical commitment to us. God has already decided—and acted upon the decision—to love us with an everlasting love, to remember us when we forget ourselves, to walk with us through the valleys of frustration and the bowels of brokenness. God has chosen to serve us with a divinity we do not deserve and to create in us a godliness we could never acquire on our own.

With God as our master, nothing is impossible, nothing is incredible, and no one is beyond salvation.

For Reflection and Discussion

- Recall and relate times when you have chosen other masters than God. How did you feel? Do the same with times when God was clearly Lord of your life. What did you experience then?

Prayer

My God, I give to you all that I am and hope to be. I offer myself in trepidation and hope, trusting that you will take the poverty of my existence and make of it a temple of your love. I ask that you help me to give this gift freely and completely, not as one who hedges bets and holds reservations. Unwavering God of love, bless my wavering devotions and bring me ever closer to you. As you do not forget me, let me always remember you, everywhere and in everyone. Amen.

Ninth Sunday in Ordinary Time

Deuteronomy 11:18, 26–28; Romans 3:21–25, 28; Matthew 7:21–27

Justified by faith and not by law

How often I have heard folks proudly pronounce, "I am a law-abiding citizen." This is their declaration of goodness, loyalty, obedience. It is also a ticket to the reward of status and acclaim. Recognized or not, there is also judgment levied with a tinge of self-righteousness. If I am a law-abiding citizen, then what/who are you? Is my abiding within the law limiting my vision? Worse yet, what does it say about the need to abide in God?

Today's readings cast a far different light and perspective on the law and what it means to obey it. Moses told the people, "You shall put these words of mine in your heart and soul, and you shall bind them as a sign on your hand, and fix them as an emblem on your forehead" (Deut 11:18). The words of the law have no effect until and unless they are first placed deeply into our hearts and souls, piercing us with God's call and commission. The law is to be a sign for us, an emblem of our journey's forward thrust.

The binding and fixing of the law upon the arm and forehead was little more than a statement of scholarly knowledge for me until one particular day when I happened to be seated in a plane near an orthodox Jewish family. We were awaiting departure. Suddenly, the father of the family arose, bringing with him a black container. He opened it, took out what appeared to be a strips of leather and a small leather box. With great ceremony and absolute precision, he wrapped the leather around his wrist and forearm and centered the box securely in the middle of his forehead. Then he wrapped himself in a prayer shawl and began to pray with whispered, rhythmic determination. Perhaps it was his regular prayer period, not to be interrupted by life's more menial tasks. Perhaps it was a special prayer for all of us that our flight would be smooth, safe, and without occurrence. I did not ask. I simply watched with interest and a sense of envy and dismay that I could not be so public with my belief.

I would be unwilling to stand before a plane filled with strangers, clothe myself with special garments that cause others to stop and stare, and then visibly move backward and forward in a unique prayer style. If I gathered up the courage to do so, my mind and heart would be filled with distracting wonderment. What are people thinking about me? Not so with this Jewish man. His ritual was revealing. He was a profoundly law-abiding Jew.

I could see that the systematically rote wrapping, unwrapping, and rewrapping of phylacteries and prayer shawl was a mantra that brought him more deeply into prayerfulness, not solely a rubric to be obeyed or a gimmick to gain attention. At one moment, his daughter bounced merrily up the aisle to tug at his sleeve. He stopped in the midst of the bobbing movement to kiss her head. Prayer, for him, was not a way to exclude people but rather a means of incorporating them with gentleness and love. He chose to bless and be blessed.

He was a man who knew his commitment to God and followed it into the marketplace where commitment might be construed as craziness. Obviously, this Jewish father listened for and heard the voice of his God and lawfully, loyally paid heed to it. He had learned that God's words remain simply words until they are put into practice, religiously but not rigidly.

For me, and perhaps for many on that plane, this Jewish father was indeed a rabbi, a teacher, for he taught me "For a person is not a Jew who is one outwardly, nor is true circumcision something external and physical. Rather, a person is a Jew who is one inwardly, and real circumcision is a matter of the heart—it is spiritual and not literal. Such a person receives praise not from others but from God" (Rom 2:28–29). He taught me that many might appear to be religious, might speak holy words and perform pious practices, but would fall by the wayside when their words and actions became troublesome for others. He caused me to question my own faith responses, or lack of them.

His prayer time was completed as the flight attendants began their initial preparation for departure. Just as quietly as he had walked to the front of the plane, he now returned to his seat and joined his waiting family.

I like to think that we all became members of his family for that time and in that place. We all had a safe, uneventful flight wrapped in the prayer shawl and phylacteries of an orthodox Jew who dared to weave and bob in full view of a plane filled with people. His presence gave us an opportunity to look again at the god we are choosing to follow. His courageous conviction provided us with a necessary reminder that God's words must be taken into our hearts, souls and spirits, not concretized into laws we can whimsically bend and twist to suit the mood of the moment. He was a living memo of the harsh truth Jesus spoke to his disciples, "Not everyone who says to me, 'Lord, Lord,' will enter the kingdom of heaven, but only the one who does the will of my Father in heaven" (Mt 7:21).

For Reflection and Discussion

- If I am a law-abiding citizen, then what/who are you? How can abiding within the law limit our vision? Worse yet, what does it say about our need to abide in God?

Prayer

Be a rock of refuge for me, a strong fortress to save me.
You are indeed my rock and my fortress;
   for your name's sake lead me and guide me,
    take me out of the net that is hidden for me, for you are my refuge
Do not let me be put to shame, O Lord, for I call on you.
Be strong, and let your heart take courage,
   all you who wait for the Lord.

                             —Psalm 31:2–4, 17, 25

TENTH SUNDAY IN ORDINARY TIME

HOSEA 6:3–6; ROMANS 4:18–25; MATTHEW 9:9–13

Faith is the fragrance that changes the world

One day as I went about the house doing chores, I noticed a television advertisement extolling the virtues of Wizard room refresher. The ad announced that this deodorizer was the fragrance that changes the world. Angels suddenly filled the air and swooped about the house. No longer would there be distasteful smells to wrinkle sensitive noses. No one would need to flee from odoriferous distress.

Smiling with amusement, I was struck with inspiration. Might this expressive ad not be a fit description of faith? I have always found great difficulty in defining faith, and perhaps describing faith as the fragrance that changes the world would be helpful. A fragrance lingers on the air long after it has left the bottle. It clings to clothing and skin, kissing it with a delightful aroma while its bouquet is being absorbed. In a way, fragrance is as much a verb as it is a noun. It perfumes while being a perfume, scents as well as being a scent.

In the gospel according to John, a verb is used to define faith, rather than a noun, highlighting its dynamism. Noun or verb, faith remains mysteriously elusive until it is exemplified in a lifetime of loving action. With the sweet smell of love, a state of being is created, one that does not pass away like the morning dew or desiccate in the heat of noonday sun. In fact, warmth releases its power and unleashes its aroma.

In other words, faith is the fragrance that changes the world!

Imbued with the scent of divinity, faithful people are called to be the fragrance that transforms the world. Our faithfulness pervades the atmosphere, rides on the breeze of incredulity, and rests on bodies of despair, scenting them with the sweet smell of feasibility.

Daily and diligently, we are people whose faith intensifies as we continue hoping against hope. We are people who look into bleak darkness and see glimmers of light, .sparks of promise. Impossibility is not in our vocabulary for all things are possible with God. Our sole concern is that we might strive to know the Lord who "will come to us like the showers, like the spring rains that water the earth" (Hos 6:3).

That kind of knowledge is found only in the mutuality of an intimate, loving relationship. Pious practices and ritual sacrifices will not suffice to deepen information to the point of integration, nor will they result in transformation. We foster knowledge of God by continuing to intensify our love of God in and with our faithful love of others.

When Abraham believed, he hoped against hope. Abraham loved God in his love for Sarah, the wife who remained barren and could easily have been sent away, according to the law. Abraham's faith in God included a tenacious trust in God's promise, despite the fact that everything in his life pointed to the absurdity of his confidence. Years passed. Sarah's infertility did not change yet. Abraham remained steadfast. "He did not weaken in faith when he considered his own body, which was already as good as dead (for he was about a hundred years old), or when he considered the barrenness of Sarah's womb. No distrust made him waver concerning the promise of God, but he grew strong in his faith as he gave glory to God, being fully convinced that God was able to do what he had promised" (Rom 4:19–21).

It was Abraham's faith that saved him—and saved Sarah. His faith saved him from the terrors of despair and the torment of disillusionment. Abraham believed in God so long and so resolutely that his faith "was reckoned to him as righteousness" (Rom 4:22). He and God were "justified." Their accounts were balanced because they were "right" with each other, of one mind and heart. The only sacrifice that could result in such at-one-ment is sacrifice lived and offered to the beat of a softened, chastened, loving heart.

This was Abraham's heartfelt love for Sarah—and hers for the husband whose commitment to her was not lessened by her inability to bear him children. His love gave life to faith. Its enduring power intensified faith into faithfulness. The fragrance of Abraham's faith changed his world, and Sarah conceived—against all odds. Vibrant life entered a womb where morbidity had taken residence. In the presence of fidelity God's promise was fulfilled.

Abraham was not alone. Noah's faithful love pointed the way to a covenantal rainbow of hope. He, too, was ridiculed. Though laughter plagued his days and echoed into the nighttime, Noah trusted. His ark of faithfulness enlarged to provide even for those who were reluctant to believe. Together, they rode the frightful floods of doubt and concern until the secure haven of holy peace was sighted—and their holiness was made real.

The faith of these pilgrims, signified in the beauty of a rainbow, was a fragrance that changed the world.

Mary and Joseph heard the call of divinity and recognized the cross it bore for them. Like Abraham, Joseph would hope against hope and defy the law in order to love the woman whose womb carried a child that was not his. Mary, as young as Sarah was old, conceived—not against all odds but quite "oddly." Trusting in God's providence—and Joseph's understanding, compassionate love and support—she went quickly to aid her pregnant cousin Elizabeth.

And once again, the fragrance of faith changed the world.

Jesus moved among tax collectors and those known as sinners because they disregarded the law. He saw them as they were and called them to what they were always meant to be—people of God. Jesus recognized their dis-ease but did not dismiss them. Instead, he shared their meal and enjoyed their hospitality. His mercy moved them to love and thus gave meaning to the law. His request was simple: follow me.

They followed, and the fragrance of their faith changed the world.

As our ancestors remained constant, loyal and obedient to God's will, so must we. As they steadfastly followed, so must we, marching beyond the rigors of law into the reliability of love.

For Reflection and Discussion

- Discuss times when hoping against hope was the only action you could take. How did you feel? What did you do? What responses or reactions did you perceive in others? How did the scent of this suffering transform you and your world?

Prayer

Dear God, so often I want to believe and am plagued with fear. So often I fear that believing will take me into places and bring me to people that will cause pain. I am afraid to suffer with your little ones. I do not wish to feel the uncomfortableness that comes with speaking a prophet's message. Help me, please, to have such a heartfelt love for you and yours that my fears will be supplanted by faithfulness; my anxiety by trust. Amen.

Eleventh Sunday in Ordinary Time

Exodus 19:2–6; Romans 5:6–11; Matthew 9:36—10:8

God is more than we let God be!

Christians carry in their core the answer to the musical question, "Is that all there is?" The answer is our resounding no! There is more to life than what we first envision, encounter, or embrace. Life is more than it seems to be. We are more than we appear to be.

God is more than we let God be!

Somehow we lose that reality in our crowded day-to-day existence. Schedules, lists, demands all subtly erode our conviction of "more-ness" and we slip into being, seeing, feeling ordinary. Problems become insurmountable and inescapable. Molehills turn rapidly into mountains. Life begins to lose its brilliant hues to drab existence. We hear it in our response: "Same ol', same ol'." Bumper stickers announce, "Same stuff…different day." There is not even the excitement of trying to survive—just a monotonous routine to let time pass.

We have all been there. We know the dull pain of world weariness. Responses become reactions, perhaps in our subconscious effort to put some zest into our being. Instead, tempers flare. Arguments ensue. And we are worse than when we began.

Into that crowded existence Christ enters. Christ is "in the pits" with us. He is moved with compassion by what he sees. His heart aches with our agony. Jesus, the Christ, feels the world's sorrow, hunger, loneliness, and bewilderment. He knows its isolation and alienation, excommunication and ennui as it is found in our individual and personal pain.

Just as his heart was moved with pity when he saw the crowds in Capernaum, prostrate with exhaustion, like sheep without a shepherd—so Jesus sees us. Too tired to fight, too tired to change, too tired to live, they and we pitch camp in the desert of ordinariness. But the Lord won't let us sink into that abyss alone. Joining us there, he sees our need to be fed and led and acts to save us. He sees that we are good. We are ready—ripe—for harvesting into the kingdom, not despite our ordinariness but because God creates out of dust, earth, ordinary material. In our neediness, we are being readied. In our weakness, as Paul writes, God is strong.

For me, the most intriguing part of the story begins here. Having seen the prostrate crowds—us ordinary people—Jesus acts by speaking to those who had chosen to follow him, his disciples. "The harvest is plentiful, but the laborers are few; therefore ask the Lord of the harvest to send out laborers into his harvest" (Mt 9:37-38).

Jesus is giving others the responsibility of gathering folks into the kingdom of God. What an awesome delegation! What a unique concept: we who are the harvest are also called to be the harvesters. In our readiness to be led we become the leaders!

Interestingly, the operative word is work. Harvesting, gathering, leading by following is work. Christ is not calling for a few good men, as the Marines do. Christ is seeking laborers. Goodness has nothing to do with it. We don't have to be perfect to be harvesters. We need only be willing workers. The rest is up to God—who is more than we let God be!

The Lord our God is a master recycler. Everyone is valuable, usable, reusable—in ways unimaginable. Ordinary people need apply. Ordinary people are called to do ordinary work extraordinarily well.

Our job description is simple: "Come, follow me." Preach, teach, heal, as Jesus preached, taught, healed. Preach the message we have heard. Teach the truth we have internalized. Heal in the manner we have experienced being healed.

What does this mean in terms of our daily encounters? It demands our bringing to mind and heart what Jesus did as he walked his way through Jerusalem and its environs. It means touching the untouchables, that is, to make contact with the persons we avoid because they are different or difficult or bothersome or annoying. It means listening and looking at everyone and everything with compassion. It means being sensitized and sensitive to the pain that crushes its bearers.

We are called to heal rather than hurt. Our vocation is to exorcise the demons of excessive guilt, shame, and futility that torment the strong as well as the weak. It is not enough to bid them go. We are called to stay with the tormented and help them calm the storm of fear and powerlessness. To be harvesters is to be forgivers, relentlessly gathering in our arms a crop which may be bruised but is worthwhile. It is to extend our circle of inclusion as we call people to discipleship—to open our arms, as Christ always opens his arms, in an embrace that is both extravagant and undiscriminating.

To become perfected in our own discipleship is to follow Jesus into the desert, pitch camp there, and listen to the voice of God saying, "You have seen how I bore you on eagle's wings and brought you to myself. Now therefore, if you obey my voice and keep my covenant, you shall be my treasured posses-sion...but you shall be for me a priestly kingdom and a holy nation" (Ex 19:4–6).

Hearing this good news elicits only one response: the gifts of life, love, truth, healing, we have received, we must give as gift. In our gift-giving all will see that "The Lord is good; his steadfast love endures forever, and his faithful-ness to all generations" (Ps 100:5).

Ah, yes...God is more—much more—than we let God be.

For Reflection and Discussion

- What "ordinary" gift has God given you that empowers you to labor in God's field and gather in the harvest? How have you touched the untouchables? In what ways have you been a healer?

Prayer

God of my ordinariness, let me see and believe that I am good enough for you, gifted enough to share your presence with others. Let me taste the sweetness of being "just an ordinary person" who is being borne on eagle's wings, soaring into the skies of divinity. Help me to let you, my God, be God and know the wonder of your generosity and abundant love. Amen.

TWELFTH SUNDAY IN ORDINARY TIME

JEREMIAH 20:10–13; ROMANS 5:12–15; MATTHEW 10:26–33

Meeting the God of light
in the grace of darkness

Jeremiah, the prophet of God, sounds like a paranoid schizophrenic in this Scripture passage: "For I hear many whispering: 'Terror is all around! Denounce him! Let us denounce him!' All my close friends are watching for me to stumble. 'Perhaps he can be enticed, and we can prevail against him, and take our revenge on him'" (Jer 20:10).

I don't know about you, but I surely have felt that sort of scrutiny and have been afraid. In fact, I still have those fears from time to time. When I express a thought, opinion, suggestion or idea that runs contrary to popular view, I hear Jeremiah's voices speaking to me and about me— and I am afraid. During those times that I stand firm in my convictions, I also await judgment, condemnation, and retaliation. Am I being paranoid or overly sensitive? Was Jeremiah? Was Jesus? Or is this the black place where I learn both the terrible perniciousness of sin and the incredibly persistent love God has for me?

The answer, for me, is obvious. Neither Jeremiah nor Jesus (nor any committed Christian) is delusional in their sense of being persecuted. They and we are realists. Sin, a clear and present danger, is real in our lives.

At the same time, it is not something we readily want to acknowledge. Sin, as we were once taught, presents itself as goodness in order to entrap us. Few, if any, of us are so perverse that we would deliberately choose overt malice. It must be covered with glitter to entice and seduce us into believing that there is some sort of good involved, even though it might be coexisting with evil. If that is true, then prophetic persons who prick our consciousness, cause discomfort, ask questions, or expand our understanding must be perceived as "good riddance."

The voices prophetic people hear; the antagonism, intimidation, and alienation they feel are not exaggerations. They are the natural consequences of our human desire to be persons who seek truth to speak truth. We want to rid ourselves and our world of falseness masquerading as truth. We want to scrape away all that has accreted and hardened us to cynicism and reveal the veracity of virtue—however vulnerable we become in the process.

If we were to end our pondering here, we'd probably give up the journey to sanctity. Who needs the grief? Who wants the aggravation? Thank God, the good news is the other—the better—half of the story. The good news is expressed in the words of the Matthean gospel, "Have no fear of them; for nothing is covered up that will not be uncovered, and nothing secret that will not become known" (Mt10:26). Hang tight and let God handle the rest.

The "darkness" that is ours as we experience Jeremiah's feelings is, in reality, a providential one. It is the place where we are especially empowered to hear God speaking to us. Our defenses are down, our dependency on God is keen, so we listen more acutely. Perhaps that is the reason that dreams are recounted in Scripture. In the darkness of sleep, there are no distractions.

The story is told about a terrible storm that occurred one night with very loud thunder, huge bolts of lightning, wind howling and things toppling over. The next morning dawned bright and clear. A terrified youngster asked her parents, "What was God doing during the storm?" While the parents were groping around for an answer, the youngster said, "I know! God was making the morning."

True though that may be, I still do not like dark places. Dark places are scary. Without illumination, familiar objects become alien traps. Night becomes interminable and I fear that morning is not in the making!

The same feelings of terror engulfed me when at the age of twelve, I was on a class trip to Riverside Park. Single file, we entered the darkness of the House of Horrors, and demonic things burst out to terrify us. I was in the middle of the line when we walked into a pitch black "snake pit" where twining creatures grabbed our feet. In my mind I saw the snakes, and I screamed and froze. Paralyzed with fear, I could not go forward nor could I have turned back to the entrance. My classmates were disgusted with me. Even the chaperone mocked me and said, "They're only ropes coiled around and made into a walkway." But I was too frightened to believe it. I had to be pushed through my panic to the exit. In the light, I was able to return to normal, but I refused to re-enter the terror.

What remains from that event is the fearful knowledge that awful things happen in the dark. That is where and when I stub my toes, trip, stumble, and fall. Feeling my way around, I curse the darkness because it has seized my power and taken away my control. A certain uneasiness overcomes me, even as I "whistle a happy tune, so no one will suspect I'm afraid."

If I am totally honest with myself, I have to admit that I learn a lot when I enter my apprehension. I touch God and let God touch me in ways that are not possible when I am in control. Amazingly, it is in the darkness that God tells me what he wishes me to speak in the light. It is in my fear, isolation, alienation, and intimidation that I learn to live a message of courage, community and conversion.

Slowly, I am becoming faith-filled. Having entered the darkness and discovered the Lord there, I am enlightened. Burdens are removed. I am free. I can truly believe that "every hair on my head has been counted." I am not afraid of anything. I am convinced that I am a valued treasure to God who creates, nurtures, and sustains me.

Now I can truly pray with Jeremiah! "But the Lord is with me like a dread warrior…Sing to the Lord; praise the Lord! For he has delivered the life of the needy from the hands of evildoers" (Jer 20:11, 13). That is the happy tune I whistle—not because I am afraid, but because I know fear and have faith in my God who meets me in the darkness.

For Reflection and Discussion

- Recall a time when you were afraid and fearful. What happened to you? How did the experience change you? What did you learn about yourself and about God from it?

Prayer

My God, I tremble with the sense of terror on every side.
I need you close as champion and guide.
My heart is faint and I am weak.
Please come to me; in whispers speak the words I must hear to summon the strength
And courage to risk life's journey—its breadth and length.
With sparrow's trust in your loving care
That holds me near and lets me dare
To hear in darkness of your great might
And speak of it in day's bright light. Amen.

THIRTEENTH SUNDAY IN ORDINARY TIME

2 KINGS 4:8–11; ROMANS 6:3–4, 8–11; MATTHEW 10:37–42

The wonder of a warm welcome

How I love visitors—when they are friends or family I know and enjoy! The company of compatriots who affirm and support, comfort and sustain, even tease and tantalize me is a pleasurable gift. I race around the house getting things ready, making meals that are easy to serve, do not demand last minute preparation, and will withstand delays. Scrumptious smells fill the kitchen and special desserts crowd the freezer. Excitement mounts as anticipation increases. Oh, how true are the words of Christ, "Whoever welcomes you welcomes me, and whoever welcomes me welcomes the one who sent me."

There is wonder in a warm welcome!

Like the Shunemian woman of influence, I urge these marvelous people to be our guests. "Come, dine with us, come, stay with us," I beg. We have room. In fact, we have two rooms set aside as holy places for holy guests, sacred spaces where the sacrament of friendship is held in reserve.

But when I do not know the folks or feel pressured by a change in scheduling or errant timing, there is a whole different feeling going on. Anxiety replaces anticipation and exhaustion depletes exhilaration. My welcoming spirit has been supplanted by thinly disguised resentment. Duty displaces desire as I am being baptized into a death I did not seek. All the careful planning turns into details that bury me in busyness. Without conscious effort on my part, anointing grace became an annoying grind. Is this what losing my life for God's sake is all about?

What is wrong?

When I look at myself and my attitude, a clear picture emerges. I love me, my choice of companions, my routine, my time frame, more than the Jesus who comes to me inconveniently, at a moment I did not select, in the form and shape of someone I do not really know. Having sought only myself, I am discovering ruin. I am learning a terrifying truth. I do not wish to take up that cross and follow an indefatigable Jesus whose mission knew no respite!

The wonder of a warm welcome is wearisome.

Too many times, in too many places, for too many people Christianity is synonymous with easy camaraderie. Many of us desire the faith that comes in "fellowship," the communion that costs nothing more than casual companionship. We want to invite to our dining table those with whom we are comfortable, not those who challenge our commitment and call us more deeply into sanctity. We ask affirming acquaintances to stay with us while ignoring those who question our values or ask that we take a second, closer look at ourselves, them—and God.

However, those unlikely, unwelcome ones are the very people who empower our discipleship. They are the catalysts for our entry into nothingness for the sake of Christ. They effect our self-discovery and promote continuing transformation.

Most important among them, is the "unwelcome self," the "me" I least like. I learn most about hospitality when I embrace my personal poverty, recognize my own imperfection, and revere my need to be interdependent. After all, it is when I am weak that I allow God to be strong! Sin, as Paul says, is my "happy fault!"

When I get upset with myself for being forgetful and cannot forgive that weakness, I touch the fallibility of those who cope with aging brains—and I learn that there is much more to life than remembering where I have put my glasses. When I am annoyed with my inability to remain calm and peaceful, serene in the midst of turmoil, I feel the pain of those whose angst has turned to vengeful anger—and I learn that patience involves suffering more than serenity.

I am the lowly one who is in need of a cup of cold water to quench the thirst I sometimes am not even aware I possess. It is only when I am truly in touch with my own impoverished sanctity that I can begin to understand my neediness and receive the richness of grace. It is then that I can honestly welcome the Christ who lives in me and choose to live in Christ's welcoming love.

I need to offer the discipleship of hospitality and service to myself—long before I consider extending it to others.

This is not self-seeking sacrifice but an authentic raising of the cross of humanity. I am to lift high that cross until I find myself involved in the crucifixion. This is not an easy task, nor is it a particularly welcome one. However it is important—in fact, essential. Arms outstretched with straining sinews express the pain and power of an open embrace.

Now I am able to love Emmanuel—God who is with us, living in us and among us—more than father, mother, son, or daughter. I am able to love the Christ who dwells in me and calls out to welcome the Christ in each person I meet. I am able to assent to the prophet I am and gain awareness of the prophet in you. Each of us can find pleasure in the company of the other, knowing both the company and its delight as holy guests. We can treasure the gifts we are, make room for them in our lives, and seek their permanent residence.

A benevolent God empowers benevolent people. In that divine milieu, there is only the wonder of a warm welcome.

For Reflection and Discussion

- What happened when you last hosted an "unwelcome" guest? How did you feel? What did you learn about yourself? What was the guest's experience?

Prayer

Christ, my savior and brother, I know you want to live your life in me. I believe that you are the welcoming host who beckons others to join our little community of two. I trust that you are my strength, my guide, my gentleness, my source of hospitality. Help me always to be openhearted and gracious to all who enter my life, bidden or unbidden. Help me to see that you are in them as you are in me. Let me genuflect before the tabernacle of their presence in awe-filled wonder. Amen.

FOURTEENTH SUNDAY IN ORDINARY TIME

ZECHARIAH 9:9–10; ROMANS 8:9, 11–13; MATTHEW 11:25–30

Humble hearts and gentle people

Can't you just hear God humming that dear old song, "I love those humble hearts and gentle people that live in my hometown"? There's a picture in my head of a smiling deity, warmed by the presence of the people called to be God's own, living in God's hometown. I can see God rejoicing heartily with the daughters and sons of divinity as they shout for joy that God is in their midst. I can imagine all of us being surprised that the God who is among us is a God who treasures humility and reveals truth to those who are open to hear it.

Humble hearts are found in gentle people who have taken residence in God's hometown.

Humility is given short shrift when it is defined as mealy-mouthed servility. Humble persons are often, and erroneously, considered to be weak—without backbone, easily swayed, quick to bow and scrape before authority. Even the dictionary does them disservice by defining humble as "low, small, slight, having or showing a consciousness of one's defects or shortcomings; not proud, not self-assertive, modest." So defined, one notes only what humility is not. Humble people are those who are not highly placed, not large, not aware of their assets. Humility is akin to humus, soil, earth.

If humble persons are those who are akin to the earth, they are basic to existence. Found everywhere, they are essential to growth and development. They are the foundation upon which gardens prosper. They give stability to what would otherwise be a sea of chaotic motion. Their consciousness of shortcomings and defects opens the way to transformation and recognition that perfection is always in the making. Not to be self-assertive, as the earth does not impose itself upon us, is to have a centrality that does not revolve around being the center. I guess one could say that humble people are like the holes in doughnuts. Unseen, they create the reality about them and keep it intact. Knowing that being oneself is the only authentic authority, humble persons are true leaders.

In my hometown, I have learned to love those humble hearts and gentle people. There is the slender, stalwart volunteer firefighter who speaks of himself as "gettin' too old to do this" but is the first on the scene at every fire call. Invariably, his sentences start with a disclaimer, "Now, y'all aren't goin' to want to hear this, but..." usually followed by a true though challenging statement. Joe is kind, considerate, compassionate, and strongly gentle. He will not veer from the right course nor will he refrain from pointing it out to those who are tending to go astray. In simple statements, he commands virtue. "Now listen, the man has a family and needs some help." Joe is not the fire chief, but he is the chief of fires, announcing their presence and racing to put them out.

Next door to us lives a man in his eighties whom my granddaughter, when she was a tiny tot of two, named Martin Bang Bang because he steadily hammered massive aluminum grills into turtle excluders. When he rides into town, it is not on a colt or donkey, but in a beat-up old truck with his little Pomeranian dog at his side. Bouncing down our dirt road, they go to McDonald's where he eats part of the hamburger and gives the rest to Ginger. Martin watches his wife live her life tied to an oxygen tank, and puts up bird feeders outside every window so that she can be part of the outdoors that is otherwise inaccessible to her. Each time my husband rearranges some portion of our landscaping, Martin drops by with a word—just one—of comment. His attentiveness encourages us.

Then there is Vernon who resides down the road a piece. At least, that is his home base. Despite the fact that he has only one leg, he is constantly on the move. From breakfasting with the local powers-that-be to keeping the books for a funeral service to advocating for better roads, Vernon is a man-about-town. Everyone knows his name. Whenever he hears of a person's need, Vernon's wallet opens generously, with nary a word spoken or a thank you expected. Anonymously he gives from all that he has so joyously received.

Lest one think that masculinity is a necessary ingredient for gentle humility, let me tell you of Mary, Vernon's wife. She is a woman who has taken her nursing skills out of the hospital environment and brought them into the community. The phone in their home has scarcely been returned to its receiver before Mary is in the car and gone to help. Like to read? Mary brings a book. Like to talk? Mary calls or stops by to "sit a spell." A "will o' the wisp" in size and unpretentious in looks, she is a giant in the land of the humble.

These are but three people among the many people who would not stand out in a crowd nor attain position or rank. But they represent those who are the earth upon which we stand. Quietly solid in their commitments, these humble folks maintain the meaning of gentleness and give credence to the power of humility.

In their constancy and compassionate caring, they exemplify for all of us Christ's call: "Come to me, all you that are weary and are carrying heavy burdens, and I will give you rest" (Mt 11:28). With their labor and refusal to despair, they have taken Christ's yoke upon their shoulders and have learned to be gentle and humble of heart. As a result, they have found rest—and now share with us all that they continue to discover. What they have received, they give as gift. With each action taken, these sainted individuals remind us to follow the lead they are following. They urge us to trust in the certitude that our souls "will find rest....For my yoke is easy, and my burden is light" (Mt 11:29–30).

I don't know about you, but every time I think about them—and all who are like them everywhere in this universe of ours—I find I cannot help but hum along with God and sing, "I love those humble hearts and gentle people that live in my hometown."

For Reflection and Discussion

- When have you felt wearied and found life burdensome? Who did you seek to assist you? Who came to your aid, with or without your request? When did you help another who was burdened? In what ways did you find rest in those actions?

Prayer

I will extol you, my God and King, and bless your name forever and ever. Every day I will bless you, and praise your name forever and ever. The Lord is gracious and merciful, slow to anger and abounding in steadfast love. The Lord is good to all, and his compassion is over all that he has made. All your works shall give thanks to you, O Lord, and all your faithful shall bless you. They shall speak of the glory of your kingdom, and tell of your power. Your kingdom is an everlasting kingdom, and your dominion endures throughout all generations. The Lord is faithful in all his words, and gracious in all his deeds. The Lord upholds all who are falling, and raises up all who are bowed down.

— Psalm 145:1–2, 8–9, 10–11, 13–14

FIFTEENTH SUNDAY IN ORDINARY TIME

ISAIAH 55:10–11; ROMANS 8:18–23; MATTHEW 13:1–23

From God's mouth to my ears

I love the phrase used in many churches at the conclusion of a particular scriptural lesson: "The word of God proclaimed for the people of God." It helps me to maintain the fact that the underlying reason to read passages from Scripture is to listen carefully to the message God is sending today to each and all of us.

What is God trying to say to me—about God's presence in my life as well as my presence in God's life? Unlike the proverbial Yiddish cry that underscores and identifies each petition and request, "From my mouth to God's ear," the proclamation of the Christian is "From God's mouth to my ear." From early morning offerings to late night examens, we yearn to hear what comes from God.

It is a good news/bad news situation. The good news is that God's word is steadfastly creative. God has promised "For as the rain and the snow come down from heaven, and do not return there until they have watered the earth, making it bring forth and sprout, giving seed to the sower and bread to the eater, so shall my word be that goes out from my mouth; it shall not return to me empty, but it shall accomplish that which I purpose, and succeed in the thing for which I sent it" (Isa 55:10–11).

When I read those words, I am greatly comforted. God is in charge of the universe and I am relieved of the strain of that responsibility. I am also greatly confused. If God's word will not return void but will do God's will, then where do I fit into the picture? Am I to simply stand by and watch? How do I participate in that creative process?

Perhaps part of the answer lies in the words of a bumper sticker I have seen: Lead, follow, or get out of the way. When I first read the message, I was annoyed. How presumptuous! The audacity of a statement that so categorized people was also insulting. With a calmer vision, I could look with the eyes of a visionary and see the command of Christianity. Make a choice—for God's sake. Lead people to God. Follow others to God. Not to choose is to take the sole remaining option—get out of the Way.

My life challenge is to be a divine cooperator. That's the work laid out for me. Obviously, it will involve discernment. What does it mean for me to be leading in God's way, following God's way, or getting out of God's way? How will I know that I am on the right path?

I guess—and that's about all I can do is to guess—that I am on the same wavelength as God, that I am truly following God's lead, being God's person, and doing God's will. Obviously my guessing must be based on empirical evidence of some sort. So I increase my awareness of my harmony with divinity by noting the music we produce together. Where I have labored to water aridity with fruitfulness, God's will is being accomplished. Where the emotionally, spiritually, or physically hungry are nourished with the bread of life, God's will is being accomplished. Where hardened earth baked or frozen to rigidity is softened with a smile, a kind word, a pat of affirmation, God's will is being accomplished. Whenever any of us bless potentiality, tilling it with trust and hoeing it with hope until it becomes an actuality, God becomes apparent.

The task is easy—if we remember to plant, sow, and distribute empowerment in exactly the manner that God does.

God is a broadcaster. The good news continues. There is no wrong place for seed to land. There is no exclusivity in divinity. Seeds are spread with deliberate abandon—and that is not a contradiction in terms! God freely and deliberately graces all creation with abundance. Goodness lies in the very act of sowing the seed. When it lands on well-travelled pathways and seems to have no effect, the birds are fed. Rocky and thorny soil still yield something, however short-lived a crop. Goodness is always given a chance at vitality. "For the creation waits with eager longing for the revealing of the children of God" (Rom 8:19).

If all of this is the good news, where is the bad?

Lack of human response is the bad news. We are our own worst enemies because we can choose to be obstacles in God's way. Our refusal to receive, share, and spread God's word will never completely nullify it or empty it of its universal power. It will, however, not produce its individual yield in a person who has no ear to hear or heart to listen or eye to see the harvest that can be had. Even more frighteningly blameworthy are those communities of individuals—especially church congregations and their leaders—whose paths are so trodden with an erroneous sense of tradition, so ridden with rock-hard rules and regulations, so filled with thorny self-importance, that God's word hasn't a chance to take root.

Their self-righteousness and sluggish hearts stifle growth. Though they appear to be looking intently, they do not see budding faith, so they scorch it with fiery fear. While pretending to listen to cries of enslavement, they do not hear. Freedom is choked—until, at last, it withers and dies.

Those who try to encourage continued development and deepening of faith, as well as the ones who seek it, find only destruction and disenfranchisement. Grave though the picture might seem, it is neither grim nor gruesome. Good news remains intact. God's word shall not return void. Like birds on the trafficked footpath, those who are rejected ingest the seeds of fidelity and fly away to a more receptive spot—a place where what is sown can fall on good soil and yield grains of faithfulness.

I have heard the stories from persecuted people, witnessed them in the lives of the alienated, and know them to be true. Wrapped in the trappings of humanity and told in tales of woe, God has visited me. Listening, I have learned to lead, follow, or get out of the way. That is the wisdom flowing from God's mouth to my ears—and yours!

For Reflection and Discussion

- How have you been a leader, a follower? When have you gotten out of the Way? What specific steps can you take to change your ways in order to be in the Way?

Prayer

Dear God, I look to the heavens and watch as rain and snow fall upon the earth, sometimes gently, at other times with a ferocity that frightens me. I look to the ground for hints of sprouting life when my own existence seems dull, dreary, and sodden with discouragement. I watch for seedlings to take hold of their bit of ground, root in it, and grow. As I wait, both in wonder and weariness, I begin to trust again that your word in me will also root itself. I believe once more that it will give me nourishment and the courage to continue. I trust that you will not let that word grow fallow or return empty to you. And I love you for being God. Amen.

WISDOM 12:13, 16–19; ROMANS 8:26–27; MATTHEW 13:24–30

Those who are just must be kind

My daughter Donna is mightily bothered by the lack of justice in the world. She chafes at the fact that employers overlook the laxity in one worker and ignore the loyalty of another. She is upset with those whose sense of equality too frequently is eroded by favoritism or opportunism. Her understanding is that good must be rewarded and evil punished. Those who are more gifted have a responsibility to use their gifts to help the less fortunate. Do your best and be your best. One neither asks for more nor requires less. This is how she treats and teaches her own children. This is what she expects of herself and her husband. Donna's view is simple, direct, and somewhat unforgiving.

When she discovered that shortcuts taken during the construction of their new addition resulted in a water-filled, unusable basement area, she began a campaign to resolve the issue. In the process, she uncovered a mess. Town inspectors were not in compliance with state regulations. New housing did not meet code. She wrote letters, made phone calls, sought legal advice. All along the way, her cry for justice grew louder.

I admire her stamina and determination. At the same time, I fear that her sense of justice may diminish her desire to be merciful. So, I keep reminding my daughter of one basic, essential reality, one reality that challenges all of us who seek the perfection voiced by the prophet Micah and required by God. That is only "to do justice, and to love kindness, and to walk humbly with your God" (Micah 6:8). What I tell my daughter is a message I frequently repeat to myself.

Those who are just must be kind.

Without kindness, justice is a guillotine that beheads what it beholds. It exposes vice without promoting virtue. Without kindness, justice is impotent.

This would seem to be the message that Jesus was trying to get across in the Matthean account of the reign of God parables. The reign of God is likened to a field of good wheat seed in which an enemy sows weeds. Wheat and weeds grow together. Each matures and yields grain. Conjoined twins, they risk destruction in separation.

In another parable, it is the hated mustard seed that takes center stage. Proverbially the tiniest of seeds, it also grows quickly in size overtaking space in the fields while providing haven for birds. Lastly, comes the image of a woman kneading yeast into her three measures of flour. Eventually the whole mass of dough begins to rise.

At first blush, these parables direct our thoughts toward the impact small entities have on much larger ones. Obviously there is a lesson to be learned in that area. No one and nothing is too insignificant in the mind of God. All are equally able to be used to do God's will in God's way. Just as important is to know that a little goes a long way.

A second look, however, would have us see the incongruity of the choices God makes. Why would God permit the integration of weeds and wheat? Why would the enemy be allowed a residence among the people of God? Is it right and just for hostility to be conjoined with holiness, maturing together, perhaps feeding on each other? Should an uncontrollable plant be left alone to grow with abandon? How about the yeast? Was it not considered to be material that corrupts? Is this apparent inequality what divine justice is all about?

God's message seems to beg our reading between the lines. There we find the paradox inherent in the call of divinity: those who are just must be kind.

The first lesson reminds us that it is not so easy to distinguish and declare what is right and good, just and fair. Most often clarity comes only after maturity. In our harvest years, when wisdom has infiltrated knowledge and given it a dose of prudent gentleness, we are better able to separate authentic grace from artificial goodness.

Hard on its heels is the second lesson: God can and does employ for service people and situations that are useless or reprehensible in human assessment. Our throwaways are divinely recycled. What we consider to be unworthy is valuable in God's eyes. There is no one who is completely contemptible or totally "trashable." We are all treasure troves of goodness awaiting discovery. Divine justice must be kind.

We are both weeds and wheat, yeast and mustard seed, with earth as our place for growth and heaven our harvest, if we so desire. God gives us all the time, talent, arena, and atmosphere to actualize our potential. Made in the image and likeness of divinity, we are empowered to godliness. As God sees, so can we. As God is, so can we be.

God cares for all and does not unjustly condemn. God's mastery over all things makes God lenient to all. Though God is the master of might, God judges with clemency. And God teaches us, by these deeds, that those who are just must be kind (paraphrase Wis 12:13–18).

This is not an injunction given solely to the saintly. It is a description of mustard seed people who grow swiftly and silently, filling the field with presence while providing food and shelter in a desert land.

It is the work of those who would be godly leaven. We are to be people who "corrupt" the world with Christianity, invisibly fermenting our environment with visible faith.

It is said that the working of leaven is plain for all to see. Put the leaven into the dough, and the leaven changes the dough from a passive lump into a seething, bubbling, heaving mass. Just so the influence and the working of the kingdom is a violent and a disturbing force plain for all to see. The action of Christianity is disruptive, disturbing, violent in its effect. (William Barclay, *The Gospel of Matthew*)

Seen and unseen, weak and strong, expressed and inexpressible, God's reign is enacted in God's way and time, through God's people. It is a rule of atonement and peace, forgiveness and forbearance. It is graciously sustained in time and over time. It is found where benevolent people perform random acts of mercy.

In other words, God reigns where the just are also merciful.

For Reflection and Discussion

- Give some examples of instances where you have been more just than merciful, and more merciful than just. What are your feelings about the kind of justice God demands of us and commands us to show others?

Prayer

God of my injustice hear my cry.
I am weak and often lie about the ways in which my mercy dies
And justice fades into revenge and retribution without end.
I want to give, forgive, forget, and lend
But tend, instead, to grab, remember, and give no heed
To the cries of the poor, the gasps of those in need.
Give me ears to hear, eyes to see, and a heart to bleed
Until justice is eased and equaled with mercy perceived. Amen.

Seventeenth Sunday in Ordinary Time

1 Kings 3:5, 7–12; Romans 8:28–30; Matthew 13:44–52

Finding our buried treasure

When the phone rang that Sunday evening my reverie was interrupted by delight. It was our eldest granddaughter calling to share some tidbits of her life. She first mentioned the ice cream cone prize she had won by correctly spelling 100 percent of her assigned words—plus the bonus word, chrysalis! At age seven she could also define and describe it for her astonished grand-mother. But that was not all.

Her next tale involved the use of a coffee can—emptied first, of course, as she reminded me—whose plastic top was slit to allow the passage of pennies. She had decided to collect these coins at school so that, when the can was filled, she could purchase a stuffed animal to be taken to the local firehouse for the firefighters to give to a little child whose house had burned down. "It's so they will have something to snuggle," she informed me. "And when I asked my principal if I could do it, she said it was a very good idea because we are supposed to be people of peace. So, guess what. I am a 'people of peace.' And I am very proud of myself."

The little "people of peace" person was summoned to bed at that moment and I was left to ponder the beauty of honest assessment. Audrey knows who she is and, like the God who made her, she is well-pleased with who she is.

I would suspect that Audrey has no problem responding to God's request: "Ask something of me and I will give it to you." Like Solomon, she is a mere youth, not knowing at all how to act yet somehow serving God in the midst of the people God has chosen for her—a people so vast they cannot be num-bered or counted. Perhaps unknowingly, Audrey has already asked God for the magnificent gift of an understanding heart—and has received it.

Unabashedly, she has touched and served those in the immediate circle of her life—her family, her principal and teachers, her classmates. But, she has also served to remind me and my husband of our sacredness. We, in turn, pass the story on to all those whose paths we cross, and they will repeat the mes-sage to their circle of friends, and they will continue it to others. Audrey has good reason to be proud of herself.

So do we—if we remember that we are today's Solomon.

When we keep in touch with our belief that "all things work together for good for those who love God, who are called according to his purpose" (Rom 8:28) we are free. We are able to walk fearlessly into the treasure we are. It will not matter much that we cannot see clearly where this journey will take us. Nor will we be tremendously bothered by the fact that we are part of a divine dragnet that contains all sorts of things, all kinds of people, all manner of possibilities. We will simply continue to be people of peace whose hearts are filled with understanding and whose covenant is solemnly pledged.

Like Audrey, we need to start by emptying our coffee can existence. First, we dispense with the grinds of life, making use of them if possible but ultimately becoming a vessel of availability. Then we slit the plastic covering that has protected us. Only a tiny opening is sufficient. Next, we offer ourselves to others. Little by little, penny after penny, one cent at a time, we allow others to donate something of themselves until we are unique containers of universal goodness. What was once simply an empty coffee can, ready for burial in a recycling bin, is now a storehouse of graciousness—an overflowing treasury to be spilled out and readied for refilling.

With each tiny contribution, our treasure grows. As it accumulates, God's operation in our lives becomes clearer. All it takes is wholehearted commitment. God does the rest.

There is an amazing byproduct gained in the process. We begin to find a buried treasure. The initial affirmation of who we really are intensifies. It dawns on us that God, from the very beginning, had given us an understanding heart. God has bestowed on each of us the ability to understand from the depths of our hearts that we are treasures. Our wonderfulness is to be emptied, shared, filled, and renewed, hidden only for the pleasure of being found.

What once we said tentatively, "I am very proud of myself," we now pronounce much more definitively. More importantly, we begin to believe that we have really been burying our treasure in false humility.

It becomes apparent that we have foolishly been trying to hide our nakedness from God. We have been covering ourselves with the kind of pride that disallows our goodness and taints our truth. We have been thinking that we were the ones to make all things work together for good. Our accomplishments superseded God's will. When the results were less than successful, lacking perfection, our faith became tenuous. Rather than daring to ask something of God and be refused, we chose silence. Instead of taking a chance that who we are is good enough for God, we remained distant and disheartened.

But now we are finding the treasure we had so carefully buried. Life's coffee can is being filled with the scent of holiness because its heart has been opened, its emptiness replete with sacrificial offerings—both our own and those of others.

In unearthing this treasure, we allow God to reign supreme. In God's reign we can relax enough to hear God saying, "No one like you has been before you and no one like you shall arise after you" (1 King 3:12).

A buried treasure has been found. We can be very proud of ourselves!

For Reflection and Discussion

- What is the buried treasure you have found in yourself? How are you sharing it with others so that they will have "something to snuggle with"?

Prayer

Creator God, you have made me in your image and likeness, an icon of love and compassion. Increase in me a desire to serve you in my service of others. Deepen in me a sensitivity to those who are needy and a reverence for those who are different from me but equally your image and likeness. Let me uncover the buried treasure that is found in all creation and let me rejoice in the discovery. Amen.

Eighteenth Sunday in Ordinary Time

Isaiah 55:1–3; Romans 8:35, 37–39; Matthew 14:13–21

Listen, that you may have life

Listening is more than an art or science. Listening is a way to be, the way to go, if we are followers of Christ, the people of God. It is interesting that the completion of public readings from Scripture are usually phrases like: "The word of the Lord" or "The word of God given for the people of God." The unstated, or understated, command is that we listen to what has been proclaimed.

To listen is to do much more than simply to hear. Listening is a process that empowers us to integrate and incorporate what we have heard into our way of living. When we truly listen, we are truly alive. Every fiber of our being is acutely aware. We are attentive to the tiny nuances in speech, the little movements of body language. We note what is said—and left unsaid. Our antennae extend. Our feelers sensitively quiver as we probe the presence of God in our environs.

I have a daughter who is the quintessential listener. She picks up every vibration and incorporates it into her psyche. It is her agony—and her ecstasy. I have never been able to hide my feelings from her because she is totally attentive to every nuance, to each change of breathe or pace. Even faceless phone communication does not elude her. If I have something to tell her that I am trying to avoid, she knows it. If I am feeling miserable and pretend that all is well, she reveals the ruse. As a result, she often carries the woes of the world on her shoulders when it is inappropriate to do so.

The wonderfulness of it all is identical. To be attuned to the spirit of all who cross the paths of our lives is a marvelous reality. When we allow the antennae of our compassion to vibrate with sensitivity to all that surrounds us, we get to know, really know, people. We are able to enter their hearts and ease their hurts as readily and powerfully as we share their joy.

When Jesus heard of the death of John the Baptizer, he felt the pain of loss. Jesus listened to that pain and heeded its call to solitude. He gave himself the gift of grieving because he knew that listening meant loving. So, he chose to withdraw, to be alone in a deserted place by himself to contemplate life without his beloved companion, cousin, and friend.

But Jesus was not the only listener in the area. The crowds heard of his departure and followed him on foot from the towns. They, too, were moved by the sound of love, a noise that filled them with awareness of their own losses. It also sensitized them to recognize the one person who could bring them solace and salubrity. Jesus is the help that heals—and somehow they knew it.

As Jesus listened to his own pain and loss, he heard the pains and losses experienced by crowds of people. As the crowds paid attention to his pilgrimage into human neediness, they were attuned to the authenticity of his presence among them. They followed someone who listened to love and loved to listen—and knew he could lead them where no one else had dared to go. They believed that Jesus would bring them into shalom, a wholeness and peacefulness that would permeate their very being. All would work for the good with the people of God. "When he went ashore, he saw a great crowd; and he had compassion for them and cured their sick" (Mt 14:14).

In the midst of this marvelous event, it would seem as if the disciples—long-time followers of Jesus, committed to his cause—would have felt they were experiencing an ancient Isaian invitation. It would seem as if a light would have gone on and an "Aha" moment would have been theirs. Could they not hear and heed their own Scriptures? "Everyone who thirsts, come to the water; and you that have no money, come, buy and eat! Come, buy wine and milk without money and without price. Incline your ear, and come to me; listen, so that you may live" (Isa 55:1,3).

Instead, they seemed able only to pay attention to their own desires. Missing the point of this powerful exercise of listening love, the disciples sought a practical closure to the day. Had they had enough, perhaps too much, of the potent potion, compassion? Was it too difficult to continue listening into the lateness of the day? Had they had a surfeit of sympathy and were they too sated to suffer anymore?

Surely, if this were the truth I can scarcely judge them. I have been that kind of disciple. I have looked around me, noted the paucity of choices, and seen that I was in "a deserted place and it is already late." My desert is often fatigue from drained emotions. The strain of day-long ministering and daily aging brings me to the lateness of the hour and of life. All I want is to be left alone to vegetate in front of the television and banish all thinking and pondering from my wearied mind. I, too, have felt that the best option would be to dismiss the crowds of people with problems so they might go to their own villages and buy some food for themselves. Let them take hold of their own challenges and leave me in peace with mine.

That, however, is not the way of Christ. If Jesus, the Christ, had a motto it might read, "One listens best who listens long and late to hear the voice of love emerge from one's own depth."

Wayfarers, those who are in the Way of the Christ, do not ask people to disperse. They give them something to eat from the great stores of grace God has already poured out everywhere and on everyone. Despite our faults and failings, no matter that the evening of life is drawing on, who we are and what we have is good enough for God—and good enough for God's people.

Thirsty, we can come to God's living waters. Without money, we receive the grain of grace and eat. Without paying and without cost we come to drink the wine and milk of God's presence. Our vision might be limited to seeing insufficiency instead of abundance. But God's view is generously creative. Gifted with divine presence we are blessed with more than is necessary for us to be tenderly attentive to our needs as well as those of others. In fact, God's promise is that all present will eat their fill and fragments will be left over, enough for yet another day.

There is but one requirement that God demands of us. One direction that must guide our journey into love. It is simple but essential, serious and exciting: "Come to me heedfully. Listen, that you may have life."

For Reflection and Discussion

- Is your attempt at growth in a relationship with God and humankind based on a frequent, if not daily, listening to God and listening for God in Scripture? In the events and situations of your daily life? Just for this day, count the times you interrupt, fail to listen, fail to hear, and fail to know and love more deeply those who are closest to you.

Prayer

O God, you challenge us to seek what eyes cannot see and ears cannot hear. Help us to keep our eyes on Jesus, to ponder his words, and to be serious about living his challenge of love. Let our words and actions be nourishment and delight for others, giving them the inspiration to love you and the courage to follow your will. So may we praise you now and in eternity. Amen.

—A Sunday Psalter ©1993 Carmelites of Indianapolis

NINETEENTH SUNDAY IN ORDINARY TIME

1 KINGS 19:9, 11–13; ROMANS 9:1–5; MATTHEW 14:22–33

Entering the world of a whispering God

I am not a whisperer. Nothing about me is silent. I am a loud Italian with laughter as my trademark. In fact, someone once commented on a dress I wore while on duty at the hospital, saying, "You won't blend in while you're wearing that dress." Not knowing whether that was to be taken as a compliment or not, I responded, "I have never blended in, not once in my whole life." So it is sometimes difficult for me to relate to a God who whispers. At least that is my first response. Then I sit back, lean back into my memories, and note the times I have whispered so that I could be heard in the midst of noisiness.

I recall my teaching days. That was a time spent with teens who marked their place in the world with raucousness. Noise was the order of the day. At first, I tried to get their attention by outshouting them, then by clapping my hands or rapping on my desk. Neither tactic worked. So, I remained silent and let the power of silence penetrate the profusion of sound. One by one, they noticed my quiet presence. One by one, they stopped talking, laughing, and jostling. Their senses no longer assaulted, my students could now hear. Together we were able to leave the sheltered nest of our own noisiness and begin our entry into the world of a whispering God.

I remember episodes from the early days of motherhood when I was young, inexperienced, and terrified of the tiny infant I held in my arms, a babe whose unending screams stiffened his limbs and turned his body red. I could not figure out what was wrong, or what to do. The mystery of infancy overwhelmed me. Intuitively, I began the age-old ritual of soothing, rhythmic, whispering sound. Over and over again, I cooed into my son's ear, "It's okay, baby. It's okay, Mommy's here." Very slowly, the screams diminished into silent sleep. Mother and son together entered the world of a whispering God.

Those memories of a life lived many years ago are no less real and relevant today when I am no longer a high school English teacher or a new mother, but a quasi-retired grandmother who spends her time writing and doing volunteer work. I have different nests of noise where I take shelter these days, but

I continue to make them my spots for retreat. I still know that I cannot remain there. Like Elijah of old, I must "Go outside and stand on the mountain before God; God will be passing by."

Today, as yesterday, there are moments when I know in my heart that God is not in the strong, heavy wind that buffets my mountain, my sturdy spot of refuge. God is not in the earthquake that splits my life in two, causing havoc and terror as everything I thought was secure turns upside-down. God is not in the fiery holocaust that inflames passionately angry reactions instead of impassioned loving response. I may want God to be there, so that I can justify my own whirlwind existence. But I will not find God there. I will only find my own fears.

God does not dwell in chaotic confusion but in compassionate creativity.

When I let the noise pass by—and I do have to allow its passage and not ignore it—then I can hear the whisper of divinity. I can leave the confines of my caved life and enter the world of a whispering God.

Jesus of Nazareth knew the wisdom of that movement and often went off by himself to pray. He left the crowds that were encasing him. He even left behind the disciples who probably drained his energy and empathy with their continuing misunderstanding of his mission. The noise of their needs and demands may well have been deafening. It might have been difficult, even for Jesus, to find God in that turmoil. So he removed himself—and sought the world of a whispering God.

The others had all had their fill. They had taken nurture from the man of Nazareth. It was time for Jesus to find his nourishment. In silence and solitude, he drew upon the strength of divinity and welcomed the wisdom he found there. It was good for him to be alone in prayer with God, his beloved Abba whose mission he was determined to fulfill.

In the wonder and mystery of this prayerful intimacy, Jesus was refreshed, renewed, and ready to return to his companions in the boat that was "battered by the waves, was far from the land, for the wind was against them" (Mt 14:24). Jesus' prayerfulness empowered him to rise above the tumult, to walk on the waves of fear that were engulfing his friends. By contrast, in their terror, the disciples could only see a ghost of a person. All the wonder they had witnessed, all the commitment they had clutched, disappeared in the night.

Fear nibbled at their shaky spirits and was chasing their faith away. It never dawned on them that God is not in the strong head wind. God is in the simple heart whisper. They gave the strength of that wind permission to swallow the whisper of their hearts. They allowed terror to replace truth.

Jesus could not leave them in that place. With the tenderness of a mother soothing her distraught babe and the wisdom of a teacher who waits until silence pierces the sound to make space for peaceful listening, Jesus reassured his friends. He reminded them of their own ability and of his continued presence that would eliminate all fear. "Take heart, it is I; do not be afraid"(Mt 14:27).

Leave the cave of comfort and take hold of the grace, the giftedness, already in our possession. Do not be afraid to stand on mountaintops buffeted by the winds of time and change. Await the passage of God—not outside us but deep within our spirit. Take a chance that God is in the tiny whispers we hear in our heart, despite the roar of those who would say otherwise.

Do not falter. Let Jesus come into our boat of human fear and watch the wind die down. Watch carefully. Listen attentively and know beyond the shadow of a doubt that God will not let us sink into the seas of our feeble faith. Our Creator is too busy inviting us to enter the wonderful world of a whispering God.

For Reflection and Discussion

- What do you think Jesus meant when he said, "Get hold of yourself. It is I. Do not be afraid"? Who is shaking your "boat" right now? In what ways do you find it difficult to stop talking so that you might hear?

Prayer

"Be still and know that I am God." (Ps 46:10)
Be stilled my spirit in quiet and peace
Slow my pace in solace without cease.
Let my silence be deep and wide
So God might be allowed to creep inside.
All noise and turmoil banished be
Leaving only God and me
To walk upon the waters of life
With nary a fear of drowning in strife.
Be still, be still, be still, and know
The God from whom my goodness flows. Amen.

TWENTIETH SUNDAY IN ORDINARY TIME

ISAIAH 56:1, 6–7; ROMANS 11:13–15, 29–32; MATTHEW 15:21–28

A house of prayer for all peoples

Every time I go to a funeral and hear the gospel proclamation, "In my house there are many mansions," I am both relieved and uplifted. It feels good to hear that God has prepared a place for us, that each one of us has a special spot in the reign of God, a personal niche readied in the presence of divinity. Apparently our religious affiliation does not deter God. Nor does our weakness and lack of perfection. There's a place for us, ready and waiting for our arrival. Only we can obstruct the works and close the door to it.

But what about now? What about this moment? Where do I fit in this church at this time? The answers to those questions do not fall quickly from pious lips—or perhaps they do, but they are not always generous words of forgiveness and acceptance. Too often, we proclaim with our lips what we neither hold in our hearts nor practice in our daily lives. Too often, our sense of righteousness is harsh and unforgiving. We join the cast of disciples who want to get rid of the people we deem unacceptable. Officiating clergy announce requirements for the reception of Eucharist that permit some while denying others. Fully cognizant of the division being caused, they—and all the pew dwellers who nod agreement—appear equally at ease with the request that we all pray for unity to occur one day!

It seems that we'd rather rejoice with a Jesus whose mission is exclusive, with a Jesus who says, "It is not fair to take the children's food and throw it to the dogs" (Mt 15:26) than a Jesus who allows the wishes of faithful foreigners to come to pass. To the first Jesus—the law-enforcing God of rules and regulations, customs and criteria—we gladly give allegiance and speak our kudos! The second one—the love enforcer—causes us pause, if not anxiety.

Why do we find it so difficult to be comfortable in the presence of a God whose house is a house of prayer for all peoples?

Might the answer lie in the fact that we have a sense, deep down in the core of our being, that we are lost sheep wandering in the foreign land of faults and failings? Despite our heritage—born and raised in Christianity, newly come to it, or still seeking the God who saves—"we are poor little lambs who have gone astray," in the words of a long-ago song. So we wonder as we wander. We seek a spot to call our own, uniquely and solely ours, in order to feel God's love with certitude.

It is not enough for us to savor the process of salvation without having certain, complete, and exclusive knowledge of the outcome. It is not enough for us to observe what is right, do what is just, and wait to see all that is revealed. We want to know right now exactly who is saved. We are uneasy with a God who promises to bring to the holy mountain of divinity all who serve, all who keep sanctified Sabbaths, all who offer holocausts and sacrifices of every sort. We are not so sure that we wish God to make foreigners joyful in our house of prayer.

We are poor little sheep who have strayed from the truth that it is God's house, not ours!

And God's house is a house of prayer for all peoples.

We have forgotten that we, too, are imprisoned in disobedience. We are no less foreigners in God's reign than are those who worship differently, pray differently, but respond equally to God's call and covenant.

It is not only an issue that separates denomination from denomination. It is a criminal offense within congregations. Each of us, in the attempt to claim our place in the Son, seems to be hell-bent in our exclusion of others. We subtly shun those who are unlike us—unless they acquiesce to our particular brand of religiosity. Somehow we are pious in our disregard and ignore the fact that they, too, are crying out to Jesus as Lord. They, too, seek the pity of their savior. They, too, are troubled by demons. We avoid acknowledgment that we all share the same humanity.

And we are eager to hear Jesus agree with us. When we are told that God's mission is only to the lost sheep of our own church, our own congregation, our own family, delight suffuses our being. Inwardly, we rejoice that God is on our side, that our way is the way, after all.

Can that be the understanding of Jesus of Nazareth? Is that how he saw the situation? Are the words ascribed to him to be taken literally? "I was sent only to the lost sheep of the house of Israel" (Mt 15:24). If so, we are forever forgotten. We are the lost sheep of the house of Christ, not the house of Israel!

Perhaps those harsh words are meant to call us to task. Perhaps they are invitations to walk in the shoes of the alienated, to know the depth of a foreigner's faith. Perhaps those words are God's way of reminding us that we, too, are exiles seeking our homeland. We, too, can do homage to God by praying, "Help me, Lord!"—and trusting that our praise is powerful despite its imperfection.

Those who are alienated ask for little, but they do ask. They are willing to be satisfied with the gleanings from the master's table. Divine leftovers are sufficient nourishment when they are denied the entire meal.

Jesus of history complied with the request for little and gave all. The Christ of faith seeks that generosity asking us to share God's house of prayer with all who ask entry. The questions remain, "If Jesus complied with the request of an unwelcome stranger, can we do less?" If we bar the door to God's house—a house of prayer for all peoples—will it continue to be God's house?

I wonder.

For Reflection and Discussion

- Who are the people who are "not welcomed" in my life? How have I barred the door to my house to them? How have I barred the door to God's house to them? If the door to God's house remains closed, will it continue to be God's house?

Prayer

Dear God, so often I feel as if I am a lost sheep. I feel alienated and isolated from the rest of the praying community because I do not think their thoughts or share their feelings. Help me to use my woundedness to heal the pain of others. Help me to recognize that my sense of being a foreigner can be salvific, if I let you be my God and truly believe that I am among your chosen ones. Amen.

TWENTY-FIRST SUNDAY IN ORDINARY TIME

ISAIAH 22:15, 19–23; ROMANS 11:33–36; MATTHEW 16:13–20

Finding certitude in uncertainty

Some days there is no difficulty at all in making profound statements of faith. When all is going well and I am upbeat and optimistic, I can look confidently at the WWJD bracelet I wear and know that God is, I am, and Jesus is running with me. My voice rings loud and clear with the passion of belief. When things are not so pleasant and I am suffering with a sinus headache or extreme fatigue, I can make the same statement. But this time, the words come forth with agonizing slowness. It is the pace, not of disbelief, but of a powerfully bare faith—a certitude that comes only within the throes of uncertainty.

When I sense that God is calling me to service and I respond to that call, only to have it denied with little or no explanation save that it is not the desire of the human mediator, my frustration and anger mount. My social worker daughter would be quick to remind me that a professional continues to complete the assigned and accepted project despite the fact that she or he will no longer be personally connected with it. I can hear her saying, "Once someone has committed to something there is no turning back or mind-changing if that person has integrity."

These are the times that try my soul and test my spirit. They are also the times when I experience the depths to which faith can take me. Only when I am vulnerable, feeling powerless and out of control, can I discover with certainty "O the depth of the riches and wisdom and knowledge of God! How unsearchable are his judgments and how inscrutable his ways! 'For who has known the mind of the Lord? Or who has been his counselor? Or who has given a gift to him, to receive a gift in return'" (Rom 11:33–35). These are the moments when my faith is a thread—but also a lifeline to which I cling.

When Jesus asked the question "Who do you say that I am?" he was asking for more than a description, definition, explanation, or identification. Jesus had already probed the inscrutability of God and sounded its depths. His faith was grounded in a trusting relationship with the God he called Abba. What he now sought was affirmation that his followers had a similar sense of the divine. Knowing that he would be entrusting them with the continuation of his own mission to save, Jesus' wish was that his followers would recognize his relationship with God and them—and subsequently theirs with him. "Who am I to you?" was a real question. Authentic witnessing rested on the answer to that inquiry.

Jesus wanted to know if Peter and the others had comprehended the fact that they would never have complete knowledge of God. They would never know with certitude how God judged or what God's ways would be. They would never be God's counselors, no matter how well they thought they had judged a situation or how many laws they could quote to substantiate their claims of righteousness. They would never give God anything but would always be the recipients of God's gifts.

That kind of uncertainty could easily lead one to a feeling of futility. If I have no assurance that I am on the right track, that my comprehension and understanding are on target, then how do I proceed? Wouldn't it be far easier to remain as I am? At least I would have the surety that I am who I am at the moment. The disciples must have had moments of severe doubt in the midst of such a radical call to faith.

However true—or false—those concepts might be, the reality is that Jesus wanted them to feel the power and powerlessness of being God's chosen ones, God's servants, God's children. Jesus wants us, today, to experience the same reality. Only in the push and pull of relationship does anyone taste and see divine goodness. Only by treading the path of blind faithfulness does one discover the presence of the ever present God. The journey begins with each individual and every community asking and responding to one primary question: "Who is Jesus and what place does he have in my/our life?"

If, in the midst of all uncertainty and wonderment, our answer is as heartfelt as was that of Peter; if we can wholeheartedly proclaim that Jesus is Messiah and Son of the Living God and prove that proclamation in prayerful action, then we are blessed. More than blessed, we are the rocks upon which God builds the church. With enduring responsibility we hold the keys of God's kingdom in hands shaking with the power of certitude in the midst of uncertainty.

It is too easy to deliver a doctrine that identifies Peter with Rock and Rock with papacy. There is little effort expended on our part when we surrender all responsibility for binding and loosing to those who are ordained in ministry and forget that we, too, are Church. We are part of the portrait of God's saving work in human history. We have and are a part of the Rock. Our discipleship is crucial to the surfacing of God's reign on earth. Hierarchical structure supplants God's plan and becomes the core of Church when we no longer believe and confess that Jesus is Messiah, Son of the living God.

In all the vagaries and uncertainties of life, one question continues to beg response: Who is Jesus to us, now, today, this moment, in this age and place? Do I name Jesus the savior of my life? Exactly what does that mean in the course of daily events? How do I let Jesus save me from myself?

The answers to these questions will always be in process, being refined and renewed as we recommit ourselves ever more completely to Christ. Life's bottom line is that I can never, entirely and surely, know the mind of God. At the same moment, I am being called always to scrutinize God's mind and will, assimilate God's call and message, sound its depths, recognize its riches and respond without seeking anything in return. In the throes of that magnificent uncertainty, I am finding the marvelous certitude that gives life meaning.

For Reflection and Discussion

- How is the prolonged, patient, prayerful, purposeful process of friendship, a friendship that propels us into the heart of another, happening to you with regard to your friendship with Jesus? How does a person's "heart identity" affect behaviors, goals, mission, lifestyle?

Prayer

My Lord God, I have no idea where I am going. I do not see the road ahead of me. I cannot know for certain where it will lead, where it will end. Nor do I fully know myself, and the fact that I think I am following Your will does not mean that I am actually doing so. But I believe that the desire to please you does in fact please you. And I hope that I will never do anything apart from that desire. And I know that if I do this, you will lead me by the right road. Therefore, I will trust you always. I will not fear, for you are with me, and you will never leave me to face my perils alone.

— Thomas Merton

TWENTY-SECOND SUNDAY IN ORDINARY TIME

JEREMIAH 20:7–9; ROMANS 12:1–2; MATTHEW 16:21–27

Celebrating the loss of labor

September brings Labor Day, a time when we Americans celebrate our ability and capability to work by taking a day off. What an interesting contrast—finding joy in working by not working! It is a concept worth examining, especially in light of the angst felt by Jeremiah in his attempt not to work for God. His labor was to serve and he believed, as do we all, that efforts are to be acknowledged in some fashion.

Humans expect that there will be some sort of recompense for our work. We will forfeit material gain, however reluctantly or easily, but in our heart of hearts we do anticipate that there will be recognition, gratitude, reward given in its stead. Without any kind of appreciative gesture, we feel duped. I wonder if that is the reason that Americans have chosen to end the summer season with a "free" day. Perhaps we have felt unrewarded and so have designated a moment to pat ourselves on the back and celebrate the fact that we do work well, hard, and often.

Jeremiah, however, gives us cause to pause and deliberate on more than reward. He asks us to ponder both the reality of working for God, serving ministerially, and the truth that such work often comes without obvious recompense and with noticeable derision. In fact, the reproach might well be a measure of our effectiveness. I know that I recoil when I am faced with uncomfortable truth. Usually first reaction is to express outrage and be fairly violent in my own defense. My second reaction is to pout in silence.

If I am successful in fending off my challenger, "he"—since it is usually my husband who is the donor/recipient of spiritual challenge—is left to respond with equal violence and outrage or to determine that he will no longer speak about the issue to me. Neither of us can sustain the enforced vacuum. After both of us have determined that we will not mention the other nor speak in their name any more, a fire begins burning in our hearts. The silence imprisoned in our bones cries for escape. We grow weary holding freedom in place. The fatigue, the futility of this prideful reaction, is overpowering. Neither of us can endure it—and so we speak. We return—not to be the persons we were but to the newly empowered and enlightened prophets we have become in the process of recognizing that God's word cannot be kept quiet. Nor can we remain speechlessly refusing to cooperate with its delivery.

Reproach, indeed, is a measure of effectiveness. Would I allow opposition, offense, derision—real or imagined—to silence the message God has given me to proclaim? Could I permit such quietude and still live a godly life?

No facile answer can be offered. To follow the Way of Christ is to walk the way of the cross. There is no alternate route, no bypass that will take us around crucial issues to ease the crunch of trafficking crowds and speed us along. In fact, to choose the bypass is to opt for the obstacle rather than the course! To offer that route to others is to be a barrier rather than a boon, a hindrance not a help. It is to be the stone in their shoe that causes both distress and distraction when we are asked by God to be the rock upon which others might stand firmly faithful.

Like Peter who remonstrated with Jesus regarding the announcement of Jesus' impending death, we often misjudge actions, choosing weakly human standards that water down and inhibit the potency of God's commands. Perhaps we fear the probability of pain. Possibly our understanding of love is shallow and superficial and that deters us from allowing faith to be fired in suffering. Whatever our reasoning, the truth lies in Jesus' response to Peter. "If any want to become my followers, let them deny themselves and take up their cross and follow me" (Mt 16:24).

Deny myself, take up my cross, and I will only *begin* to walk the Way of Christ! This seems to be mission impossible—until I respond to one imperative at a time. The first order is to deny myself. That is easily a daily occurrence—and it is a prime experience of paradox. Choose Christ not me and I will lose the great "I am" and find the true me! No doubt the choice will hurt a little, maybe a lot, but the prize is worth the pain.

Take up my personal cross—the one fitted to my shoulders and weighted enough to exercise my faithfulness. In the denial of self, I have already picked up the cross. No need to look around for it! Now to carry it over the footpaths of fear, onto the mountain of fidelity where death is conquered and resurrection happens.

There is no ending to this pilgrimage, only beginnings. Always there will be new beginnings, extended horizons, stretches that slightly exceed one's grasp. To follow in Christ's footsteps is to be ready for continuing surprises along the journey into life. If there is effort involved, it is the energy demanded of us as we engage in the work of loving and allowing ourselves to be loved. It is to toil in God's vineyard without counting the cost. Toil is the oil that propels us.

Happily duped by the God who calls us into divinity, we follow in the steps of our savior. We also discover that we can and must celebrate the loss of labor in discipleship because ours is a graced voyage, blessed not by what we do but in who we are!

For Reflection and Discussion

- Discuss what it means to deny self. What value does that action have in your life? What do you think of the statement, "The false me might be my cross"? What crowns have you seen in your life that came as a result of the crosses you bore?

Prayer

Dear God,
Help me to walk by faith and not by sight.
Let my life bear me to valleys deep, but light.
Take me beyond my wildest dreams
To your presence, your plans, your schemes.
Bring me delight in every tear,
Profound joy where there once was fear.
Carry me close, embrace me tight
As crosses cause me to clutch in fright.
Deepen my trust that you are my true prize
As I travel from my "deaths" to rise
And know that I am graced to be
Just the person you wanted to see. Amen.

It pays to pay attention

If ever there was a call for a listening, loving, softened heart, we hear it clearly in today's Scripture passages. We have all been summoned by God to be attentive, to be alert and sensitive to the voice of God. Our vocation, collectively and individually, is to deepen awareness of the God who has saved us from death and drawn us into the circle of divine life. Life's wonders, set before us, are gracious and free. The only cost is to pay attention.

Hearing is often a painful process. Sometimes we strain to catch sounds in the midst of thundering noise. At other moments, what is audible is so loud that we cringe with distress. Listening goes one step further. I can remember standing at my kitchen stove, stirring a pot of spaghetti sauce, when one of my daughters asked me to listen to her. She began her sad tale about something that was disturbing her and I, facing the stove with my back to her, kept on stirring. She fairly shouted at me, "You're not listening to me!" Equally annoyed at being reprimanded I retorted, "Yes, I am. You just told me that...." And I proceeded to repeat verbatim the words she had spoken—only to get her angry reaction: "Yes, but you are not listening. Stop stirring that sauce and look at me!"

Because I could repeat what I had heard, I thought I was paying attention to her. It never dawned on me that my continuing the task at hand was a clear sign to my daughter that my hearing was impaired by inattentiveness! What mattered more at the moment was efficiency—doing two things at the same time. Dinner's preparation and daughter's problems were equally weighted. Indeed, my ears were hearing her words as my eyes watched that a simmering pot did not boil over, but I was not listening with my heart. I had not understood that dinners can wait when daughters cannot.

We have spoken of that incident many times since it occurred. The incident continues to serve as a graphic reminder to us of the necessity of attentive listening. How can I warn others for God? How can I be a watch person for the people of God if I do not really hear God's word?

Those questions should haunt us. They should pursue us as we noisily travel life's paths. For we are nothing if we are not listening lovers, tenderly listening to Love's voice speaking through each other.

Our "bottom line" is a simple one. "The one who loves another has fulfilled the law." To have acted out of love toward my daughter those many years ago was to have put down the serving spoon, turn around to face her, and give her total attention. Am I more attentive now that I was then? Or am I still bound by the law of efficiency, of getting my agenda done well and on time? I would suspect that many of us guiltily face those accusations. We do evil with good intentions—and sometimes "good" with evil motivations.

It is interesting to me that the Scriptures record Jesus saying to his disciples, "If another member of the church sins against you, go and point out the fault when the two of you are alone. If the member listens to you, you have regained that one" (Mt 18:15). Forgiveness, reconciliation, depends on communication. Confession commands confrontation. That is the challenge of being watch persons for the people of God. If I have been sinned against, I cannot stand by silently stewing with anger. I must speak. I must talk to my brother or sister about the hurt, anguish, sorrow, and downright sin that has been levied upon me. I cannot afford to ignore the evil that is done. If I "do not speak to warn the wicked to turn from their ways, the wicked shall die in their iniquity, but their blood I will require at your hand" (Ezek 33:8). Having spoken, I must wait and listen, listen and wait.

To love is not always easy, nor is its way smooth. Love's burden, its agony and its ecstasy, is freedom. Love listens and leaves the other free to respond or refuse. When the effort to open all avenues of communication has been made to no avail, both parties are bound with words spoken but not heard. The result is tragic. Ever higher walls are built; ever wider breaches are opened. Individuals now ignore each other or treat one another with less than common courtesy. Each attempts to avoid contact with the other, leaving both bereft of healing presence.

Deafened to the spoken word, unable to listen, we find that it becomes difficult to love oneself and impossible to love one's neighbor. The heart hardens and the community hurts. Two or three may continue to gather together, but it is no longer truly in the name of God. God is there in the midst of them—remaining unrecognized, unheard, unattended. Instead, each person is busily stirring his or her own spaghetti sauce. Each is able to repeat words verbalized and heard but never turns to face the other with love, never listens to the message of the heart.

The God who listens remains steadfastly present, shackled by the immensity of our human freedom to choose. Indeed, we bear a tremendous responsibility. Our ability to respond is mightily freeing as well as masterfully restrictive. We have the power to hear—to listen, learn, and love. We also possess the potency to remain deaf—to turn our backs on truth, knowledge, and compassion. We can bind people with rejection and refusal or set them loose them with acceptance and affirmation. We can gather together as a community to listen to the Lord in our midst or drift apart in isolation. The most frightening statement of all describes the vast effects of our choice: "whatever you bind on earth will be bound in heaven, and whatever you loose on earth will be loosed in heaven" (Mt 18:18).

There is but one prayer, one plea, begged for us by those who are our prophets, "O that today you would listen to his voice! Do not harden your hearts" (Ps 95:7–8). If you have no prophet in your community, I'll lend you my daughter. She will tell you the challenging truth: "You're not listening!" Turn, face God, and listen!

For Reflection and Discussion

- Share some episodes and incidents that indicated you were hearing but not listening, present but not attentive. What did you learn about yourself? What did you discover about the person speaking to you? How did those experiences affect your understanding of prayer as communication?

Prayer

God of my hardened heart, I beg that you might soften me enough to hear the beating of my own heart. Hearing, may I then pulse with the beat of the heart of those with whom I live and work and play. Help me to have the courage to go to my sisters and brothers with whom I have difficulty, those who have injured me, intentionally or not. Let me speak to them with love, tell them of my pain, and wait attentively to hear what they have to say to me. Give me the grace to accept them as they are and the strength to be forgiving. Amen.

Twenty-fourth Sunday in Ordinary Time

Sirach 27:30–28:9; Romans 14:7–9; Matthew 18:27–35

Forgiveness is forever

No one ever said that Christianity was an easy course to take. Nor has it been reported that one who consistently and continually claims God as master has smoothly sailed through life. Probably the biggest obstacle in the path of all who would seek sanctity is the need to be eternally forgiving. Humanly, we ask for limits. Seven, seventy, seventy times seven—let's count it up and total the cost, sum up the payment due. Then we'll be able to calculate risks, make decisions, and go on our way.

The Way of Christ is far different. There is no quantitative bottom line. All that exists is quality, a manner of living that exists in forgiving. The obvious reward is reconciliation. When we forgive others, we are better able to forgive ourselves—and become more open to acceptance of God's forgiveness. In that cycle of giving and receiving, atonement happens. At-one-ness with God occurs. Our life and God's is in sync. We are reconciled.

Each time I struggle with my "unreconciled" bank statement, I am painfully jerked into a real encounter with a similar spiritual experience. In my mind's eye I can picture God going over the numbers of times I have missed the mark, looking to find where the errors have occurred, erasing the event, re-entering the correct figures until God's statement of truth and mine are the same. What joy and relief there is in reconciliation! It is well worth all the time and effort spent going over the facts and figures of life.

Now to transfer the information and process to my relationship with others—there is the rub. When the encounter is only between God and me, the pain involved in searching for my errors is tolerable. The end result delights. As soon as I am asked to participate in the same endeavor with my companions in life, I forget my own omissions to concentrate on theirs. I strive to be the punishing God who relentlessly seeks the fault without remembering that divinity also denies retention. God's pencil has more eraser than lead—but not mine!

With God, and therefore with us, forgiveness is forever—or it is nothing at all. Despite the fact that we may recoil at the thought that we are called to be forever forgiving, the reality is "anger and wrath, these also are abominations" (Sir 27:30). Only sinners hold them tight. Only the foolish avoid recognition that those negative feelings do more harm to the holder than to the recipient. While I allow myself to remain filled with wrath and anger against another person, there is no room for mercy and patience with myself. Before I know it, my angry self will not permit forgiveness of any sort—including mercy toward my own failings.

I recall my father's advice given to me and my husband twenty years ago. We were not youngsters entering into a first marriage with starry eyes and fanciful dreams. One would think that advice was unnecessary. But my nearly ninety-year-old father thought differently. He peered at us from glaucoma-ridden eyes to say, "If you want to be happy, overlook the little things and forgive a lot." His near blindness had forced him into contemplation of time lost and energy drained in the futility of choosing not to forgive. Recognizing that loss, he wished us to be avoid falling into that trap.

Forgiveness is forever. The happiness of freedom is its reward.

If I nourish anger against others, I cannot expect healing from God. When I am totally absorbed in nurturing the negative, I can neither acknowledge nor accept anything positive. I am not free! I guess we all need to ask ourselves some important questions: "How will vengeance prove to be a benefit for me? What will happen to me if I cloud remembering with revenge?"

Everything in life has a price. Each of us needs to comprehend precisely how costly are the consequences involved in occupying ourselves with the task of holding others bound. It is a labor of loss, not love. No one wins at this game.

Forgiveness may appear to carry a high price because it demands patience, forbearance, compassion, and concern. The difference is that we are enlarged by the cost, not diminished. As we give, we grow. As we are emptied of the need for retribution, room is made for our replenishment. Slowly, it dawns on us that we are all debtors, all are indebted to each other in ways that render us unable to repay. We cannot remove our own bonds without breaking the bonds of others.

Our grace is not in trying to get from others what we ourselves will not give. Our grace is in recognizing that all of us are in debt to the God who has told us that we are free to love divinely! Everyone is indebted to a God who loves generously, graciously, and endlessly.

We are free to accept a life where God is master, not ourselves. We are free to be responsible to God by responding to the needs of others. We are free to treat our brothers and sisters in exactly the same way that God treats us.

The question remains, "Will we choose to accept that freedom and forever be persons who forgive from the heart or reject it and be bound eternally, confined in our own prison of relentless retaliation?" Each of us must respond personally. All of us are divinely empowered because, God knows, forgiveness is forever.

For Reflection and Discussion

- In what ways does holding someone bound through lack of forgiveness inhibit both your and their freedom? How costly are the consequences involved in retaining this kind of bondage? How is it a "lose-lose" situation?

Prayer

O God, strength and friend of the forsaken, we praise you in Jesus who bore the burden of our sins with a forgiving heart. Help us to walk in his spirit. We know a world of pain and anger that dots our history with war and division. Teach us how to respect our differences and to forgive as we have been forgiven. Give us the grace to realize the unity for which Jesus prayed. We ask this in his name. Amen.

—*A Sunday Psalter* ©1993, Carmelites of Indianapolis

TWENTY-FIFTH SUNDAY IN ORDINARY TIME

ISAIAH 55:6–9; PHILIPPIANS 1:20–24, 27; MATTHEW 20:1–16

It's not fair, it's right!

At best, life is a mystery to be celebrated. At worst, it is a problem to be solved. In either case, it is a topsy-turvy world of surprises. It is the experience of living with a God who is inscrutably transcendent. At the same time, this God holds out the ultimate promise of intimate presence—"I am the Savior of all peoples. Whatever their troubles, I will answer their cry, and I will always be their Lord" (*Entrance Antiphon*).

If I can count on nothing or no one else, I can count on God's availability and assistance. However, I will never be allowed to be complacent in this relationship. Never will I be able to take God for granted and lapse into lukewarmness, thinking that I have a handle on the God of Surprises. This is the God who teaches us that the core of life is love and the center of love is justice. Perfect love is found in total justice; perfect justice is discovered in consummate love. Interestingly, equality—as we usually understand it—has nothing to do with love.

I can remember my grammar school days, a time when I was rapidly gaining weight. My mother tried her best to help me change my eating habits. Though well-meaning, her efforts were unsuccessful because I thought I was being treated unfairly. I became angry as I watched my younger, frailer, and much thinner sister receive larger portions than I. Seething, I thought to myself, "It's not fair!" And then I used my own pocket money to buy potato chips. On the way to school, I'd consume the whole bag to even the score, to procure justice. That would teach them all not to treat me unfairly!

As long as I busily sought equality with my sister, there was no way I could find justice and love in all that my mother was trying to do for me. My thoughts were not those of my mother, nor were her ways mine. Unable to enter her mindset, I denied myself the surprise of a healthy, thinner body because I wanted to be treated identically to my sister, despite our different needs. I ignored any possibility that my mother was doing what was right, for me as well as my sister.

Those days are long gone, but the urge for that false sense of equality persists. How often do I yet look at others with envy and want to have what they have or be who they are! I see only what I can see, know only what I know—and make determinations, not always accurately, based on those perceptions. Is it not true for nations as well as individuals?

On a trip to the Holy Land, I was struck by the presence of armed guards and security checkpoints, especially in a city that was already walled and had been for centuries. Arabs, Palestinians, Christians, Israelis—all vying for equal space and ignoring the justice of perfect love. There seemed to be no thought of peaceful co-existence in this land filled with holy places and praying people. I could feel the earth itself crying out for a shalom that was being denied by humans desiring overpowering equality instead of omnipotent justice.

Jesus' parable of the kingdom of heaven likened to a landowner looking for laborers comes vividly to mind. We—individuals, communities, nations, alike—make our contractual agreement with God. We accept God's terms and commit to life with God, along with its subsequent demands and rewards—and feel special, privileged, useful, and worthy besides. Everything is fine until we begin to notice that others are joining our ranks. Any problem we have with that understanding is suppressed and coated with the belief that our reward will be proportionately greater, decided according to the time and effort we have given to the task of being good. We resent God's equality, which is based in generosity, and seek only our own, bound in legalism.

But God promises only one thing: "I will give you what is just."

God will not cheat us or treat us unfairly. God will give us what we need, what we agreed to accept, what is right for us to have—nothing less, and usually more. We can count on it! If God chooses to give us more, there can only be celebration of divine graciousness. If God chooses to give everyone more, it is none of our business! Freely God gives and freely we receive—that is the essence of justice.

We can choose to grumble, sulk, take our pocket money, defiantly buy our potato chips, eat the whole bag by ourselves—and miss the surprise of justice. Or, we can decide to "love one another and come to perfection in the eternal life prepared for us" (Opening Prayer A). The acceptance or rejection is ours alone. God will not reject us, confine us, bind us, or leave us idle all the day, with no care for our well-being. God calls each of us, sending us to do what we can do, when we can and how we can. Ours is but to respond, taking note of our own commitment without comparison to or contrast with that of others.

To do otherwise is only to limit ourselves, for we can never limit God! In the entrance antiphon for today's liturgy we hear the words, "I am the savior of all people. Whatever their troubles, I will answer their cry, and I will always be their Lord." The expansiveness of this promise is astounding. No one is eliminated; all petitions are heard and answered. Always God will be Lord— even when we refuse to acknowledge or acquiesce to that rule!

The foreverness of our God boggles the mind. Generously surprising and surprisingly generous, God's promise has been made and will not be retracted, no matter how much we might moan and groan about fairness and equality.

Divine rule is not fair. Thank God, it's just!

For Reflection and Discussion

• When have you experienced the difference between justice and equality? How did it affect your self-understanding? Have you ever experienced your personal rendition of buying and eating a whole bag of potato chips in angry retribution for unequal treatment? What happened?

Prayer

Dear God, I find it so hard to see others being treated in ways that I wish were mine. I want to love them as they are. Let me know that my repentant "no" is no more virtuous than another's unfulfilled "yes." I want to see and seek justice instead of inequality, but I am weak and fail so often. Teach me to love as you love. Teach me to be grateful and not grasping, delighted, not discontented. For this I pray. Amen.

TWENTY-SIXTH SUNDAY IN ORDINARY TIME

EZEKIEL 18:25–28; PHILIPPIANS 2:1–11; MATTHEW 21:28–32

Attitude is everything

Do you remember being required to tell your brother or sister or little friend that you were sorry for the way you acted? Can you also recall the next phrase that came from your parent? "And say it like you mean it?" Simply saying "I'm sorry" was never enough. It was necessary to have an apologetic attitude. Essential then and crucial now is the sincerity of our sanctity. Neither words nor actions alone are sufficient.

It's all in the attitude!

Paul phrased it rather succinctly in the demand he placed before the people of Philippi: "Let the same mind be in you that was in Christ Jesus" (Phil 2:5). There it is, in a nutshell. To call ourselves Christian, we must also command and convey the attitude of Christ. What we say or do rings falsely if our attitude is less than godly. It is as simple—and as complex—as that.

The simplicity lies in the fact that those who follow Christ cannot be ambivalent. When we say yes it must be with unyielding conviction, just as it must be when we say no. Mediocrity is more than a mistake. It is malevolent. Its complexity is found in our experiences of the God whose ways seem unfair. Yet our God would rather we were steeped in sin than be stuck complacently in "halfway holiness."

That statement always makes me pause. As outrageous as the notion appears, it simultaneously soothes and stirs me to an understanding that life becomes more complicated when I strive for the simple sole-mindedness found in Christ. No longer can I rest easy by following the trail of unexamined justice. Henceforth, I must decide to seek the ways of God, ask to be guided in truth, search for radical humility—and act accordingly.

How wonderful it is to know that God delights in our wholehearted decision. How awesome to discover that God can do more with and for us in the rigidity of our rejection than in wavering virtue! It is neither heat nor cold but the lack of either one that offers dismay to divinity. Why else would Jesus say to the chief priests and elders, "Truly I tell you, the tax collectors and the prostitutes are going into the kingdom of God ahead of you" (Mt 21:31). Sinners in God's reign before "professionally perfect holy persons"? What a frightening thought! Where are we in that analysis?

If we put on Christ, all is seen differently. As a result, we are able to act responsibly with real virtue. Judgment, justice, and revenge give way to forgiveness, mercy, and compassion. Debts are not counted as bills for which payment is due. Instead, the obligation owed is to give each other encouragement and support. A completely new understanding of fairness applies. We begin to ask ourselves, "Is it God's way that is unfair—or ours?"

It's all in the attitude!

Once we have integrated a Christic attitude, it becomes abundantly clear that we are "in the form of God." Humans made in God's image and likeness, when they truly realize their depth, do not grasp at divinity to hold it jealously close or take exclusive ownership. Instead, we empty ourselves of our divinity in order to be more accessible to others. Our attitude makes allowances. It gives us the opportunity to choose to be bound to other humans so that, together, we might become free.

No longer can we be enslaved by rivalry or conceit. Because we have "the attitude of Christ," each of us looks to others' interests rather than our own. Life is other-centered, not self-centered. Ours is the attitude of one who saves and soothes, consecrates and consoles, comforts and challenges, each given as needed in appropriate doses. That is our existence—and our exaltation.

It's all in the attitude!

Only persons who take a strong stand can assimilate Christ's attitude. Make no mistake about it. Those who think holiness has the hallmark of weakness are sadly misinformed. Openness to the workings of God's spirit demands a certain vulnerability—not one of weakness but one that permits divine entry. In a profound sense, we control God's passage in our lives. We limit God's working because we are the gatekeepers of our souls. Only I can say "yes" or "no." No one else can do it for me. Many may plead in my behalf, push or prod me to go this way or that, but I am the sole arbiter of my fate. When God asks me to go and work in the kingdom's vineyard, I choose. I may respond positively and act negatively. I may respond negatively, regret it, change my mind, and do God's bidding. God waits. I decide. My decision is based on my attitude.

If I have truly "put on Christ," the cross will loom large in my life. It is not a case of choosing and then sailing on smoothly. To opt for God is to find life in death-dealing situations. Nothing will be easy, but difficulties will be greased with grace. We will be empowered to see into life's experiences so that we might have vision beyond them. It is not a matter of offering up hardships so much as it is rising through them—gaining altitude via attitude.

I guess the "trick" is to remain focused on divinity without noticing our successes or failures. Stay on the Way. Get in the Way. And always concentrate on life's "way-ness." Live in the process while believing in the product. This is more than going with the flow of things and floating willy-nilly in a river of circumstances.

To live in the process of faithfulness is to have an attitude of awareness. It is not to grasp at grace but to gasp at gracefulness. Only then will we truly see God's ways as fair. Only then will we taste and see God's goodness. Only then will we honestly repent, return, and believe unwaveringly that God shows us where we may find life and know it abundantly.

It's all in the attitude!

For Reflection and Discussion

• In what ways have you controlled God's passage into your life and limited God's working in you? How have you sought to empty yourself of your divinity in order to be more accessible to others? How do you understand the statement, "God would rather we were steeped in sin than be stuck complacently in 'halfway holiness'?"

Prayer

God of my prideful attitude and false humility, teach me your ways. Help me to recognize that my repentant "no" is no more virtuous than another's unfulfilled "yes." Keep me from acting out of rivalry or conceit and let me see my own graciousness so that I might more deeply appreciate the goodness of others. I ask this in the name of my companion and savior, Jesus, the Christ. Amen.

Twenty-seventh Sunday in Ordinary Time

Isaiah 5:1–7; Philippians 4:6–9; Matthew 21:33–43

Tenant farmers in God's garden

When I first read today's Scripture selections I was confused. Both the Isaian and Matthean passages seemed to present a picture of God's powerful judgment from which there is no recourse. I could almost hear the voice from heaven booming: "Do what I say—or else!" The words echoed some of my less enlightened parenting days. I thought, "Is this what God is trying to convey?" Is God a "do-or-die" sort of parent? Am I called to hear, heed, and obey a deity who offers no freedom, whose fundamental and commanding order is summed up as "My way or the highway!"?

Paul's letter to the Philippians—his "chosen people"—offers a different view. He encourages them—and us—to "Do not worry about anything, but in everything by prayer and supplication with thanksgiving let your requests be made known to God. And the peace of God, which surpasses all understanding, will guard your hearts and your minds in Christ Jesus" (Phil 4:6–7). Which is the more accurate portrait? Are they both to be believed? What is going on here?

In my confusion, I put away the Scripture readings for the moment. Well, what I really did was put the book down and let the Scripture begin to seep into my marrow! Who is this God? What is the message? The questions became the subject of prayerful pondering and meditation.

Slowly, the fog lifted from my spirit. I began to realize that God is asking me—and you, as well—to respond to a divine predicament. God is seeking our comment on his concerns: "What more was there to do for my vineyard that I have not done in it? When I expected it to yield grapes, why did it yield wild grapes?" (Isa 5:4). Imagine that! God is asking us humans to see things from God's perspective and then question ourselves accordingly so that we might take appropriate action.

I felt more at home with that understanding of God. It brought to mind the many summer days when my husband would come into the house, mid-afternoon, all sweaty, dirty, and frustrated because the garden was not as productive as it should be. He, too, would give me an Isaian "divine litany," saying: "I have spaded, cleared it of stones, planted the choicest seedlings, removed the weeds, watered it, fed it blood meal, bone meal, and wood ashes. I don't understand. What more could I have done?" Like God, he expected a good crop because he had given good care!

I then would respond with soothing reminders that he had done his best. Though he toiled with the causes, the effects were not in his control. He could not make growth happen. He could not prevent all predators and weeds from invading and killing his plants. He could only watch, wait, and continue to work. But my gardener husband would not be consoled. He returned to the garden, uprooted the unproductive plants, and placed them elsewhere to see if they would grow in the new soil. Daily, he walked in his new garden area and communed with his transplants. He and his garden were intimately connected. Its yield was his yield.

I watched and thought, "Isn't this what God is doing in our lives?" God plants, waters, feeds, hoes, pulls out weeds—and expects us to yield a good crop. But there is more to the story. We are both garden and tenant farmer. We are the yield of God's efforts as well as the caretakers of the garden kingdom.

What a response-ability!

Gardens have but one purpose: to respond to the gardener's loving care by yielding a bountiful crop. Gardeners have but one goal: to care lovingly for their plants so that the produce might be fruitful. For both garden and gardener, harvests are the inevitable judgment. That's pressure. That's anxiety. The questions abound, whether stated or silent. Will I glean enough to feed my family? Will there be more than we need so that I might sell some and make a living from the land? Ultimately, the uncertainty focuses on the wondering: "Is this all worth my time, energy, and effort?"

For God, the answers are always a peace-filled "yes" to all the above—but perhaps it will demand a change in the gardeners or the garden being moved to a new locale. Time, energy, talent, funds, and effort are expended no matter where the garden grows!

That thought frightens us, for we are tenant farmers. We are accustomed to staying in one place with one crop. Perhaps we'll plant by rotation each season to rest the soil, but we scarcely move beyond our comfort zone. We who call ourselves the people of God often respond with less than divine spontaneity or peace. Our "shalom" comes primarily through prayer-filled action. We need to plant good seed and tend it well. We need to follow Paul's advice and make certain that "whatever is true, whatever is honorable, whatever is just, whatever is pure, whatever is pleasing, whatever is commendable, if there is any excellence and if there is anything worthy of praise, think about these things" (Phil 4:8).

In other words, the garden will grow and so will we if the Son is shining in our lives. There will be a rich harvest of peace beyond all understanding, the peace that only God can give. There will be justice for all. There will be an attitude of gratitude.

The wonderful truth is that no matter where it is, no matter who tends it, no matter what must be done to achieve a bountiful harvest, God will have a garden! We have a simple choice: to be with God or against God. Our choice is our judgment. We will be planted anew or uprooted. We, the tenant farmers, can only stand in awe-filled prayer, proclaiming: "this was the Lord's doing, and it is amazing in our eyes" (Mt 21:42).

For Reflection and Discussion

- What is the state of your life garden? How have you tended it, spaded it, allowed it to be fertilized with God's grace? In what ways have you resembled the property owner who leased his carefully planted vineyard to others? Or are you more like the tenant farmers who would not release a fair share of the vintage crops for fear that their portion of the rich harvest would be diminished?

Prayer

Sometimes, my God, I feel like a forgotten garden. I feel trampled, neglected, plucked of all my gifts and talents. In my anxiety, I pray that you will take care of what you have planted in me. I trust that you will look down from heaven and place gardeners in my life who will tend my hurting spirit with care and compassion. Trusting, I will dismiss all anxious thoughts with prayers shot through with gratitude. I believe that you will see that I am a rich harvest for you, a vineyard of vintage grapes and virtuous grace. Thankfully, I pray. Amen.

Mountaintops are seductive

One of the most thought-provoking accounts I have read during the past few years is the description of a Mount Everest climb. It was interesting to note that reaching Everest's summit, exhilarating and challenging though it might be, was only part one of the adventure. Contrary to what one might believe, leaving the mountaintop and returning to base camp was an even more frightening venture than getting up to the mountain's top. The reason the departure was so fearsome had much to do with dangers that accompany the exhilarating feelings of achievement and success discovered in reaching the pinnacle.

Mountaintops are as seductive as they are stimulating.

Peaks, though they are goals, can never be conclusions. The excitement of arrival too easily saps both the physical strength and the psychic energy need-ed for descent. Tremendous willpower is necessary to "gear up" for the down-ward trip. Timing is of utmost importance as well. Climbers must leave the summit while they still have sufficient light or they will be traveling in dark-ness where missteps can be fatal occurrences. Companions are essential. Though one always experiences a mountaintop alone, other people are neces-sary for safe passage both en route and returning. Finally, the key to a satisfac-tory outcome is perseverance. To give up can mean death.

Spiritual mountaintops are quite similar events.

Peter wanted to build an encampment on the Mount of Transfiguration so that he could maintain the wonder of it all and remain in the glow of the moment. Jesus disallowed that idea. He reminds us—that is, Peter and all who have followed him—that mountains are to be climbed, enjoyed, relished as good. Mountains are to be remembered in our careful descent. Mountains are not permanent perches.

Dr. Martin Luther King, Jr.'s understanding of the mountaintop was made ever-more poignant in his thundering speech in which he repeated the cry, "I've been to the mountain!"

Isaiah underscores these remembrances with yet another:

On this mountain the Lord of hosts will make for all peoples a feast of rich food, a feast of well-aged wines, of rich food filled with marrow, of well-aged wines strained clear. And he will destroy on this mountain the shroud that is cast over all peoples, the sheet that is spread over all nations; he will swallow up death forever. Then the Lord God will wipe away the tears from all faces, and the disgrace of his people he will take away from all the earth, for the Lord has spoken. (Isa 25:6–8)

On Mount Zion of old as well as the summit of our spirituality today, we know (in a manner different from all other times) that God is most generously God. We see quality and quantity wed in the Lord's abundant love. We believe that God will destroy all those veils of ignorance, hatred, malice, jealousy, envy, spite, pride, and greed. God will remove all the heavy curtains of separation that we have allowed to keep us in darkness, preventing the entry of light into our lives. All that has brought and continues to bring death to communities—be they comprised of two persons, ten, or thousands—will come to an end. Tears will be wiped away as reproach is removed. Life, not death, will reign! This we believe with all our heart—especially when we are on the mountaintop!

To be effective in the long term, however, mountaintop experiences must be internalized. Daily perseverance is required. Peak experiences cannot survive as one-time invitations to glory. They must come alive in steadfast responses to the kingdom calls given each day of our lives. Masked in ordinariness and disguised as annoyances, they come. The phone rings annoyingly right in the middle of our most favorite television program—and we are summoned to discipleship. We settle in for a relaxing afternoon, interspersed with a nap or two, when a neighbor knocks on the door to ask for help. God is visiting. A hard-of-hearing, elderly relative who tells the same boring stories containing constant complaints and criticisms asks us to come for coffee— and we are called to feast with the Lord.

Do we refuse to answer the phone or go to the door? Or do we respond graciously? Do we ignore the invitation or accept at all costs? Do we go merrily along our way—or God's?

Faith finds its depth in faithfulness. And faithfulness is discovered in persistence.

Paul says, "I know what it is to have little, and I know what it is to have plenty. In any and all circumstances I have learned the secret of being well-fed and of going hungry, of having plenty and of being in need" (Phil 4:12). The days when we can echo his sentiment are the times that the mountain peak is inverted and becomes the depth of our tenacity. As the pinnacle pierces our veiled existence, our faithfulness is revealed. It is no longer important, nor does it even matter, whether we eat well or go hungry—are well-provided for or do without. Our whole focus will have shifted to a core creed: "I can do all things through him who strengthens me" (Phil 4:13).

Only through faithful discipleship will we recognize the invitation to come to the banquet. Only through perseverance will we be ready to eat at the table with all of God's invited guests. As we come down from our mountaintop, carrying the memory with us, we are fitted with the garments of glory. We become holy people of God living our "yes" to the Messianic banquet prepared for us and singing praise to the God for whom we had looked all along the way.

Let us rejoice and be glad that God has saved us! For, we have been to the mountaintop, we have experienced the Lord and are alive to tell the story until we and the mountain are one.

For Reflection and Discussion

• In the past month, how have you responded graciously to God's call as it came via annoyances? What specific steps can you take to deepen your response and increase your availability? If you can, describe a particular mountaintop experience you have had in the course of your life, one that evoked a desire to pitch a tent and stay there.

Prayer

Dear God, I sometimes wonder if I even know what a mountaintop experience is. I judge my peak moments against those of others and fail to see any height. If I want to stay there, it is often impelled more by inertia than excitement. Help me judge the depth of my being rather than the height another may attain. Let me know that you are with me in the descent and you will lead me to the ultimate base camp where all will gather to share the story of our journey until we and the mountain are one. Amen.

Twenty-ninth Sunday in Ordinary Time

Isaiah 45:1, 4–6; 1 Thessalonians 1:1–5; Matthew 22:15–21

Goods cannot become gods

There is great wisdom in the saying, "The more things change, the more they stay the same." In the midst of our best efforts it seems we remain pitiably human in our mediocrity and disregard of the exalted divine image to which we are called. This was true of Israel, God's chosen people, who lost sight of their commitment to God's service in their race to gain political power. It became the reality of Paul's divided community at Thessalonica. This flawed human nature became enfleshed in the entrapment question put to Jesus by the Pharisaic and Herodian plotters. Sorry to say, it is also the case today.

God calls us by name to be his people. We respond fervently and affirmatively to the privilege—and promptly forget what we said. More importantly, we forget who God is! We get caught in the same trap plotted for Jesus as we ask, "What can we give to Caesar and still be 'legally' good?" Basically, the problem is that we are asking the wrong question for the wrong reasons. Perhaps that accounts for Jesus' clever response recorded in the gospel according to Matthew!

If we look at Paul's letter to the Thessalonians and the gospel account as parts of a dual approach, we might see a "good guy/bad guy" routine in operation. In other words, Paul does a magnificent setup for Jesus' sharp retort. The communities obviously differ in time, geography, and space. However, they in their time and we today share an identical challenge of discipleship.

Paul knows the Thessalonians' difficulties regarding faith and lifestyle while awaiting Jesus' second coming. He is also aware of divisions in the church community. Therefore, he begins his attempt at healing them by laying down a series of affirmations. "We always give thanks to God for all of you and mention you in our prayers, constantly remembering before our God and Father your work of faith and labor of love and steadfastness of hope in our Lord Jesus Christ. For we know, brothers and sisters beloved by God, that he has chosen you" (1 Thess 1:2–4).

Essentially, Paul's methodology was to remind the Thessalonians of their call. He did for them what Isaiah did for Cyrus the Persian. Both were echoing God's message of personal, divine selection. "I call you by your name, I surname you, though you do not know me. I am the Lord, and there is no other; besides me there is no god" (Isa 45:4–5).

Who we are and what we do or achieve as Christians has nothing to do with our abilities or efforts. Indeed, who we are and what we accomplish has everything to do with God and God's gracious presence enlivening all creation.

How difficult it is for up-by-the-bootstrap, independent North Americans to internalize that fact! We parade our degrees, positions, backgrounds, and experiences as proof that we are people who can achieve. It shouts to all who care to listen that we are the ones to be chosen.

God calls our bluff by extending the invitation to others, giving them titles and arming them, as he did Cyrus. What is God trying to tell us? Is it that we are unable, unworthy, ignorant, ill-prepared? Or is it that God is valiant in the effort to convey to us that we are not in charge?

We are not ever asked to be in charge—only to respond to the charge we are given.

Being in charge and having control, being busy about many things is the modern coin with which we pay our worldly taxes to Caesar. Those are values held dear in business, government, social, and educational systems. The more "in charge" we appear, the more control we seem to exercise. The greater our degree of busyness, the more successful we are—by Caesar's count. Life is lost in the tossing of a coin—a coin whose head and inscription is Caesar!

If cartoon strips are any indication of reality, this is a piercing problem. In the Scott Adams creation, *Dilbert*, a performance rating was portrayed. Alice's boss stated that she had "met expectations" during the preceding year and was due a two percent raise. Alice was indignant, considering the fact that she had worked eighty hours every week, earned three patents for the company, and given bone marrow (not once but twice) to their biggest customer. All her efforts were considered to be "expected." Sharing her dismay at lunch with her companions only added to her troubles as she heard one of them saying, "I told you the bone marrow thing would haunt you." From another came, "I'm starting to think the time I worked through lunch was for nothing." Caesar wins again!

So what is a person to do? Stop working and begin begging? Again, wrong questions are being asked. The answer has little to do with working or not working. The answer is found in Jesus' simple statement: "Give to Caesar what is Caesar's."

There is no problem with being an effective, efficient, organized, zealous worker. "But give to God what is God's." The second part of Jesus' comment gives perspective to the first. It is sort of a backward sentence. Give to God what is God's. Start here and everything else falls into proper place.

The call we have been given is to be people for whom there is no Lord but God. Accumulation of wealth, nice homes, cruises, volunteer work, even "church jobs" are all goods which cannot become gods. In a most insidiously seductive way, the good we do can become the god we worship. It courts us and calls us by name, gives us both title and power—and we never realize what is happening.

Danger remains unless we consciously give to God what is God's. Give to God all that we are and do, daily and with great discernment. Painstakingly examine our motivation, keeping an honest assessment of labors in love. Give to God first, totally and with complete conviction, and Caesar will automatically get his due. Our lives will be in balance. The preaching of the gospel will prove to be not a mere matter of words, but one of complete conviction carried out in the power of the Holy Spirit.

Give to God what is God's and goods won't be gods!

For Reflection and Discussion

- How does your life experience resonate with or deny the statement that our modern coin to Caesar is to be busy about many things, in charge and control of all? What examples can you give that illustrate that the good we do can become the god we worship?

Prayer

God of my "busyness" let tranquility reign
Give focus to my scattered self and ease to my pain.
Offer me questions to ask, not answers to proffer
Allow my hardness to melt, so that love I might offer.
Empower my sight, chase blindness away,
Make my hearing acute and compassion a mainstay.
Open my heart to the power of my name—
Child of God be my only acclaim.
I return to you what you gave to me,
Wonder, awe and goodness beyond degree. Amen.

THIRTIETH SUNDAY IN ORDINARY TIME

EXODUS 22:20–26; 1 THESSALONIANS 1:5–10; MATTHEW 22:34–40

Show and tell in the kingdom of God

When Robert Fulghum's book *All I Really Need to Know I Learned in Kindergarten* hit the bookstores, people chuckled at the poignant humor, and copied verses for future reference or timely remembrance. What Fulghum gave to a tired and disenchanted world was a primer for good education based on the familiar words: show and tell.

Preschoolers first experience that approach to learning with their tales of intimate family stories and experiences. Elementary pupils hone the practice as they embellish those episodes with exaggeration for effect. High schoolers perfect it with sophistication—labeling it "lab work." Adults continue the process, though we do not refer to it in the same way. Instead, we both search our genealogies and consume libraries of "how-to" tomes. Whether it is for veracity or variety, we all want to show and tell something to someone at some time.

There are moments that alternate between showing and telling. Other times it is a consecutive movement. Still others are simultaneous actions. Fulghum writes that we do as we teach: "Warm cookies and milk are good for you." How often have we eaten as we spoke those words! Again, "When you go out into the world, watch out for traffic, hold hands, and stick together." Even hardened urbanites bearing years of experience hold hands and stick together in the traffic of life. We also see this philosophy in the kiss of peace at liturgy. We show as we tell and tell as we show. Life and learning then emerge more powerfully than ever we imagined.

What Fulghum failed to note—and what we too often forget—is that God is both the first and the ultimate show-er and tell-er! God does what God asks of us: Show me, as I have shown you. Tell me what I have already told you.

From the opening creation story in Genesis to the final episode of Revelation, there is a recurring theme. We are continually being asked to prove that ours is a committed response. At the very same time, God consistently models this convicted response for us.

God's is the perfect show that tells.

God speaks and creation is done, proof of the effectivity of the divine word. God makes good on the divine promise to be with creation always. God is present when Abraham faithfully agrees to sacrifice his son—and Isaac's execution is permanently stayed. God promises freedom from slavery to the Israelites and fulfills it by leading them out of Egypt to the Promised Land.

No matter how far people stray, God remains with them—to cajole, to lead, to provide opportunities for growth, change, and choice. Always there is choice. God shows the divine presence, whether it be in howling wind, booming thunder, lightning flashes, burning bushes, gentle breezes, or angelic messengers and challenging prophets. Ultimately, the demonstration of who God is and what God wants comes to us in the person of Jesus, the Christ, who then shows us the way to serve and wait, wait and serve.

God shows us how to live in the divine image and likeness. We know who we are to be and what we are to do because it has already been exemplified for us. God has already proven his goodness, kindness, omnipotence, generosity. God's expectation is clearly announced through Jeremiah, the prophet: "This is the covenant that I will make...I will put my law within them, and I will write it on their hearts; and I will be their God, and they shall be my people" (Jer 31:33).

This is the statement of a God who wishes to possess us completely. It is the law of total belonging to a God who has given us all that can and should be given. What we have been given, we are now commanded to return as gift. God has loved us with an everlasting love. God has called us and we are God's. God's ever-present care for us is enfleshed in the great commandment of freedom that empowers us to love our neighbors as we ourselves have been loved—with an everlasting love.

Why do we make it such a difficult task? Why do we persist in trying to trip God up? Why do we continue to question the "greatness" of God's command? Whatever the explanation, the fact remains that God will never stop reminding us of our heritage. We are persons made in the image and likeness of a God who is love.

We humans, one and all, must model God's love. That is the way of our life—the only way in which we can find life. It is the basis of every code of law. To do anything other is to invite our death. We ourselves are the wielders of the sword that kills!

Not only does God hear the cry of our impoverished psyche, but God promises a reward. We are given security in the joy of the Holy Spirit. We are guaranteed divine solace. We can trust in the fact that there is light in every tunnel, even when we fear facing the darkness. The joy of the Spirit is not a fleeting feeling of happiness. Spirit-joy is a continuing presence that makes possible all that seems to be impossible, even loving the unlovable ones we encounter. It is the support that empowers us to stand in opposition to this world's agenda.

In a society that worships youth, beauty, and intelligence, we serve the old, disabled, and handicapped. In a world where money speaks volumes, we offer a plain life, rich in all that God freely gives. We hear the cry of the poor and answer them. In other words, we are the "show and tell people" described by Paul in his letter to the Thessalonians. "And you became imitators of us and of the Lord…so that you became an example to all the believers….For the word of the Lord has sounded forth from you…in every place your faith in God has become known, so that we have no need to speak about it. For the people of those regions report about us what kind of welcome we had among you, and how you turned to God from idols, to serve a living and true God, and to wait for his Son from heaven, whom he raised from the dead —Jesus, who rescues us from the wrath that is coming" (1 Thess 1:6–10).

We are Lovers of God. How we love is the show from which we tell absolutely divine stories.

For Reflection and Discussion

- In what ways have you shown your family and friends that God loves them with an everlasting love? How have you loved your neighbor as yourself? When has this been difficult to do?

Prayer

Dear God, some days I can scarcely love myself much less anyone else. There are times when I do not want to show or tell anyone anything. I want to imitate Christ who loved no matter the cost. I want to be creative and nurturing, giving life and spirit to those who are lonely, sad, and needy. But I cringe at the infringement on my time and energy, and so I cry out to you to hear me and be compassionate. Remind me of my own lovableness so that I will be strengthened to reach out with love to others. I know you hear me as I pray. Amen.

MALACHI 1:14–2:2, 8–10; 1 THESSALONIANS 2:7–9; MATTHEW 23:1–12

Gentleness is the hallmark of God's priestly people

Over the years, my husband has persistently posed the question, "Why don't you try to be more gentle?" Just as doggedly I reply, "Because I am earthy, not gentle." However, I am profoundly aware that my response begs the issue, offers an excuse but not an explanation, and leaves me with a nagging feeling that I am avoiding a very important growth factor. I am somehow evading the necessity of taking everyday efforts to direct my steps on the path of gentleness—the gentleness found in a nursing mother who cares for her children.

I am filled with awe at the sight of mothers with babes at the breast. Such peace, calm, care, and deep love is conveyed as mother gazes upon her child and child caresses mother in return. They breathe in unison, it seems, each heart beating as one. Contentment pervades the air around them. No matter the sacrifice of time or energy, the treasure of this communion, this sharing of self, is worth all cost. At this feeding moment, the child knows only its mother; the mother only her child. Concentration, devotion, thoughts, feelings, are focused on their togetherness. Nurturing is the sole desire. When encouragement is needed, it is given in crooning word and melodic line. Otherwise, silence is the song they sing. Smiles are their spoken words.

If only I could maintain this picture in my heart as well as my mind, I would easily be able to look more closely at the changing mood of my own humanness and see clearly the limits which my failings impose on hope. I would recognize that faith gives us the promise of peace and makes known the demands of love. I would pray for the removal of the selfishness that blurs my vision of faith.

Indeed, gentleness is the hallmark of God's priestly people.

Gentle persons know well how to proclaim the gospel of God without laying burdens of guilt, shame, impossibility, or uniformity upon their listeners. Gentle persons are hearers of the word long before they are its bearers and speakers. They are the people who have integrated God's commands into their lives in the manner of a child at its mother's breast. They and God's word are in communion, breathing together, hearts beating as one. What they are experiencing, they practice. What they practice, they preach—without fail or fear.

Becoming gentle in mind and spirit is hard work. One might say, as Paul did to the Thessalonians, that it is "our toil and drudgery." Night and day we must labor and learn, in order to maintain the holy balance of challenge and comfort, disturbing without destroying. The task is sometimes frightfully demanding. Repeatedly we lapse. Continually we pick up and begin again. Wearisome, tedious, it is a necessary effort because we easily fall prey to the heady desire for power and prestige.

It is far too comfortable for us to make harsh demands on others while evading the responsibility of compassion and companionship. Despite our coy dismissals of praise, too often our works are performed to be seen. We widen our arena of authority until there can be no incorporation of another's ideas, talents, gifts—nor is there any recognition given them.

Before long, partiality is shown in the decisions we make, the people we choose, the prayers we voice. Those who agree with us become important; those who disagree, disappear. Unity is buried in a grave of conformity to all that we have perceived to be right and good and in keeping with our understanding of God's will. It is only a short time before we forget that we all have one father, one God has created us. Next, "we break faith with one another, violating the covenant of our fathers" (Mal 2:9–10). Instead of enhancing faith we empower fear and futility. Rather than encouraging healing speech, hurt-filled silence happens.

Indeed, gentleness is the hallmark of God's priestly people.

We are all ordained to be gentle people. Dire consequences result when we refuse to obey and refrain from any attempt to transform our overbearing authoritarianism into overwhelming authenticity. Those who continue to bully others into submission, who "tie up heavy burdens, hard to bear, and lay them on the shoulders of others" (Mt 23:4)...who "will not listen, if you will not lay it to heart to give glory to my name" (Mal 2:2) are given fair warning. The Lord of hosts says, "I will send the curse on you and I will curse your blessings" (Mal 2:2).

The words we speak will soon become stale in our mouths. They will echo off the walls of power we have built around us. Like boomerangs, they will return to confront us with our own hypocrisy. Eventually the truth will emerge—for our redemption, reformation, and re-creation.

No longer need there be only the choice to exalt ourselves by humbling others and laying unnecessary burdens on them. The struggle to be first—to have places of honor, public greetings and acclamation—is replaced by a profound sense that God is working in us, through us, and with us, if we allow it to happen. We can acknowledge that God is the source of all good in everyone, everywhere, and all the time. We can rejoice in sharing ourselves in the same way that a mother nurtures her child.

Touching and being touched by the wonder of mutual presence, we can become God's people. We can affirm and accept our vocation as individuals and communities ordained to proclaim God's word and work, live generously the faith we profess, and walk gently along the path of life.

We are priestly people. Gentleness is our hallmark.

For Reflection and Discussion

- When have you broken faith with another person because of bias, prejudice, or personality conflict? What experiences have you had of being oppressed? Of having heavy loads placed on you by others who refuse to help you carry them? How have you done the same to others?

Prayer

Jesus, my brother and savior, you carried the cross for me and gained victory through your death and resurrection. Help me to carry the cross God has given me, no matter the cost in blood, sweat, and tears. Give me the grace to recognize the heaviness of another's cross. Show me how to lend a shoulder in help, an ear to listen, and a gentle hand to wipe away tears. Let me learn who I really am and who you really are in my life and humbly rejoice in the knowledge. I ask you this with praise and grateful thanksgiving. Amen.

Thirty-second Sunday of Ordinary Time

Wisdom 6:12–16; 1 Thessalonians 4:13–18; Matthew 25:1–13

Looking at life through the eyes of the wise

As I ponder the problematic parable of the wise and foolish virgins, I remember basking in the dubious afterglow of my sixty-fifth birthday celebration. My then eighty-eight-year-old mother delighted in reminding me that I was now on her side of the mountain—the slippery downward slope, to be exact! Has wisdom accompanied me on this treacherous trek through life's adventures? Or have I remained among the foolish?

The gospel today begins with a terrifying stark statement, "Then the kingdom of heaven will be like this. Ten bridesmaids took their lamps and went to meet the bridegroom. Five of them were foolish, and five were wise" (Mt 25:1–2). Everyone is starting out on equal footing. The universal attitude is one of welcoming and waiting. All took their torches with them—the light that would illumine both the bridegroom's way and their own. No one would stumble around in the darkness. So far, all is well. But, the story quickly veers into a scene where separation is highlighted. Of the ten bridesmaids, only five were sensible. Only five noted the possibility of difficulties or dangers and prepared as best they could. The remainder seemed oblivious. Their expectations, though lovely, were limited. Their capacity for surprise and their ability to cope with delay were similarly handicapped.

I would have expected Jesus to have described God's kingdom as one peopled only with those who are wise. Not so. Both wise and foolish ones populate the reign of God. Prudence and patience, sense and sensibility walk hand in hand with a falsely charismatic spontaneity that lacks preparedness The underlying question deals not with the reality of our life in God but with the manner with which we live in God's reign. What is our perception of divine life? Is it a proactive response to grace or a reactive one?

I reside in the retirement area of the South and am surrounded by many sage people. Despite the many experiences I could relate concerning their wisdom, there is one example of sagacity that has me spellbound. It is the story of my own personal "Charlotte"—a spider, like the one in the book *Charlotte's Web*, that I have grown to know and love.

My story begins with an evening encounter. My husband had opened our sliding door and was just about to meander onto the deck when he gasped with astonishment and backed into the living room. Directly in his path was the most magnificent—and the largest—spider web he had ever seen. Feverishly working its maze was an enormous and energetic arachnid.

Though I turned on the porch light at various intervals throughout the evening, trying to catch her (I decided the creature must be female) in the act of ensnaring her unwitting victims, I never saw anything more than busy preparation and quiet anticipation. With each illumination, there was only a spider clinging to a web that billowed gracefully in the nighttime breezes. Carefully crafted, the silken threads did not break nor did its core resident fall from her central post. She did nothing but wait. My Charlotte was at the ready for her surprise. When morning dawned, there was nary a sign of her presence. No web remained. Perhaps, if I looked carefully, an anchor thread or two might be floating as indicators of what had been but was no longer. Had her "bridegroom" arrived? Had she been awake to meet and greet him?

That will never be mine to know, I guess. All that I know for certain is that she is back—in the same spot and at the same time each evening. Charlotte keeps her nightly vigil with lamps burning and oil to spare. It does not seem to perturb her that morning's light reveals no indication of her existence or of her labyrinthian labors. In her wisdom, she knows that her life is not marked by what she produces. It is tallied in the efforts she makes. Consistently and persistently, she does what her spirit calls her to do. Charlotte weaves her web. She is who she is called to be—simply spider! Tearing down and building up are the cycles of her sanctity.

Holding on to the center, no matter how the wind blows, is her vocation. What comes her way—when and if it does—remains a surprise for which she is both ready and readied. Even my watching is not an intrusion. Noticed or not, I become part of her evening chore. I am incorporated into the wonder of the web. Without doubt, I am never a cause for arrested activity. Charlotte continues without pause, weaving with faith and waiting in hope.

Those moments spent contemplating my spidery friend are opportunities I have been given to look at life through the eyes of the wise. In what ways do I resemble this creature who allows nothing and no one to interfere with her mission to be who she is and do what she must—or die? Is the web of my life one that is anchored yet open to the breezes of God's spirit? Am I solidly ensconced at its center, holding on for dear life to the divine core from which all emanates and to which all leads? Do I await, with clear faith and deep trust, that I will be fed during the nighttime of dark improbability?

I have learned a great deal from my Charlotte. And I am continuing to be consoled by the message she bears. "To fix one's thought on her is perfect understanding…because she goes about seeking those worthy of her, and she graciously appears to them in their paths, and meets them in every thought" (Wis 6:15–16). Not a night will go by that does not speak of God's graciousness interwoven with my own humanity.

It is the web that weds—a divine network allowing me to look at life through the eyes of the wise.

For Reflection and Discussion

- In what ways do you resemble this creature who allows nothing and no one to interfere with her mission to be who she is and do what she must—or die? Is the web of your life one that is anchored yet open to the breezes of God's spirit? Are you solidly ensconced at its center, holding on for dear life to the divine core from which all emanates and to which all leads? Do you await, with clear faith and deep trust, being fed during the nighttime of dark improbability?

Prayer

Lord Jesus, in the days of your ministry, you listened to women and followed their counsel. You sent a woman to tell the news of your resurrection to your followers. Grant us the insight to let the fruits of your Holy Spirit flow freely through every member of the people of God, so that we may all share in the life you have gained for us. We ask this through the intercession of all your saints who died longing for the coming of your reign on earth. Amen.

—*A Sunday Psalter* ©1993, Carmelites of Indianapolis

Proverbs 31:10–13, 19–20, 30–31; 1 Thess 5:1–6; Matthew 25:14–30

Wedded to God

Today's readings seem to be so disparate as to make one wonder about the reasons for putting them together. There is the marriage imagery of Proverbs—with its emphasis on the role of women, work, and reward—followed by a Thessalonian endtime warning and the Matthean account of unused talents. Could it be that we are being invited to reflect upon the meaning veiled in two distinctly different but equally valuable and connected realities?

First is the fact that we are wedded to our God. Divinely "husbanded," we are worthy, valued beyond pearls, entrusted with the very heart of God who considers us to be an unfailing prize. Full of light and love, we are children of the day—radically optimistic, filled with joy to our core, yet soberly alert and aware of the temporariness of this life.

The second reality is the consequence of this relationship. Because we are who we are—God's people, living a commitment that is no less sacred than marriage vows, our call is to fearsome faithfulness. Ours must be a loyalty that is devoid of fearfulness and filled with awe. We are people to whom much has been given, with a trust that the gift will be well used. This, for me, is unsettling because it hints of evaluation, judgment, being found lacking. I get my dander up and ask, "What's the matter with me as I am? Why do I have to change...do more...be more?" I begin to agitate with the thoughts that I might never reach the expectations of this challenging God to whom I am wed.

I am feeling uncomfortable, disconcerted, shaken, and disturbed. Annoyed with my feelings, I am becoming disgruntled with the God who has caused me to feel them! I am afraid of this demanding God who won't leave me alone to remain securely attached to the "me" I am comfortable with. I try to hide from this God who won't let me say "I can't"—and leave it at that!

God has given me everything I need. God believes in me. It is I who have chosen to respond to that faith with fear.

Does that diminish the demands of divinity? When I think about that question, I also think about the persons in my life who have made demands on me, those persons who love me so much that they will not allow me to be less than I can be. Nor will they allow me to stagnate in any one stage of my life without asking me to look beyond where I am to see where I could be.

I remember a conversation I once had with a priest friend. He was looking through a liturgical calendar when he noticed some Advent wreaths. Pointing to them, he looked at me and said, "You could make those." My immediate response was, "No, I can't. I know the extent of my talents and artistic creativity is not one of them." What I received in return was a raised eyebrow—a sidelong look. No words—just a knowing look. More that slightly perturbed, I stared right back at him. Without warning the words popped our of my mouth as I said, "I don't want to learn that I have any more talents. I have enough to handle right now." Now, that was the truth!

I was afraid that I would have to be more...do more...change more. All I wanted to do was go off and bury the gifts I had been given in the ground of self-imposed limitations. I wanted to escape from the challenge of becoming and run from the risk of failing. I wanted to remove the burden of responsibility and remain secure in the complacent belief that I had given enough—more than enough—of myself, without stretching to give more.

I was burying more than my giftedness. I was burying myself—in fear!

I am fortunate—we are fortunate—to have, in God, a friend who "husbands" us with "knowing looks" that evoke growth. God believes in me...God believes in you...and asks only that we believe that we are, all of us, divinely gifted persons. Called to such faithfulness, the only appropriate action we can take is to use our giftedness responsibly.

Given life, we need only to share it, believing that sharing is already causing an increase of life within us. Given forgiveness, we need only be forgivers to discover that forgiving expands our ability to love and care for others. Given peace, we need only use the wholesome spirit of that shalom to dispel violence and promote understanding. Given patience, we can suffer ingratitude, anger, and hostility—to learn that compassion grows with the suffering.

To use our giftedness as human persons is to learn truth. God reaps where God did not sow. God gathers where God did not scatter. Neither sowing nor reaping, scattering nor gathering, God uses us to do that work. We are handed the divine work of creating...redeeming...healing...loving. As well, we share the joy of being God's cooperators. To use our giftedness is to grow more humane and become more human. In the process, we discover what Anthony Padovano states in his book, *Belief in Human Life*:

> It is no easy thing to be a human being. A human life is the most unforeseeable and dramatic venture imaginable. The risk of living increases in direct proportion to the quality of life. An animal can never be less than

animal. It is destined to grow and die with the perfection of its senses rather than the definition of its identity, at issue in its living. A human life is radically different. No one knows what a child will become. Transformation is at issue in human living. In all of this, there is risk, a measure of failure, and yet the possibility of becoming someone who transcends himself/herself and all limitations.

Being a human person is no easy matter. To be human is to "belong neither to darkness nor to night; it is not to be asleep like the rest, but awake and sober" (1 Thess 5:6). To be human is to recognize that we have been given both divine life and the limitless possibilities of God's presence. If that were not enough, the awesome fact is that we will be given more and more—until we are rich in the life and spirit of our Creator God.

Only one question remains.

Will we risk the demands of being wedded to God—of living in that richness? Or will we choose to bury ourselves in fear and chance losing even the little we have?

For Reflection and Discussion

- In what ways have you risked the demands of being wedded to God? How have you chosen to bury yourself in fear, chancing the loss of the little you have? Who has been a catalyst to your spiritual growth and how has that person affected your life in God?

Prayer

Creator God, I thank you for the graces you have bestowed upon me, especially the gift of being entrusted with the very heart of God who considers me to be an unfailing prize. I am sorry for all those times I have failed to appreciate and use those treasures, the times I have turned my back on grace, turned toward fear, and failed in my faithfulness. Come to me, ever more assertively, in my weaknesses so that I might know your strength and return to you with fuller graciousness. In Christ's name, I pray. Amen.

FEAST OF CHRIST THE KING

EZEKIEL 34:11–12, 15–17; 1 CORINTHIANS 15:20–26, 28; MATTHEW 25:31–46

Dance in the shadow of death and discover God's reign

Today's readings are both comforting and challenging. In a sense, we can almost see Jesus talking to himself as he is immersed in that divine process.

How dare I say that and what do I mean? Well, it is quite interesting to note that this section of the Matthean gospel comes as a conclusion to a trio of parables concerning vigilance, wisdom, creative living, and preparedness. Jesus appears to be reviewing his own earthly ministry in light of Ezekiel's oracle regarding the reign of the shepherd king. Additionally, he is previewing his role as judge on the heavenly throne. However, both past and future are connected by the present existence in which he is walking into his own passion and death. Resurrection will follow, but first the pain of passion and dying. This is underscored in the very next chapter of Matthew's gospel beginning with Jesus' statement: "You know that after two days the Passover is coming, and the Son of Man will be handed over to be crucified" (Mt 26:2).

From our first breath of life, we begin dancing in the shadow of death.

That is the solemn movement of Christ's kingship and the rhythm of our own walk in his way. Challenge number one is contained in that same mysterious journey. The summons is to consider the critical question: "How do we balance life in the midst of death, and death in the core of life?" Balance! That is the key issue. When we lean too far in either direction, we risk a fall either into a cockeyed optimism that defies reality or a paralyzing pessimism that denies it.

How do we accomplish the balance? Perhaps the best response rests on attitude rather than specific activity. There is no definitive check list of things to do. There is only the constant honing of our consciousness. Another way to put it is to adopt the hospice philosophy: live until you die. Terminally ill patients are keenly aware of death's presence. Many of them choose, with great deliberation, to live at death's door and dance in its shadow. There is no denial in their choice, nor is there euthanizing euphoria. There is only profound reality. Like them, we need to look death in the eye and say, "I know you are here, but you don't have me in your clutches. I am going to use your presence to help me come alive. You will be my memory of past events, good and bad, and my mirror into ever new possibilities."

The second challenge emerges from the first. If we choose to live until we die, what is our focus, perspective, and viewpoint on living? It seems to me that Jesus plainly tells us: "Live in me as I live in you." According to Teihard de Chardin, this is being in the divine milieu. For Paul it was: "It is no longer I who live, but it is Christ who lives in me" (Gal 2:20).

Christ lives his life in me. Christ lives his life in you. When we are lost, God is lost. When we stray, God strays with us. When we are injured, God is wounded. In our sickness, God is ill. All that God is, with us, we are called to be with others. We will be judged on our servanthood among the flocks of God's people.

Now my balanced life-in-death is raised to the ultimate. The challenge of judgment day clearly has less to do with what I have or have not accomplished than it has to do with recognizing Jesus alive and living his life in each of us. We will all be judged on our sight more than our insight. The critical question will be, did we see that Jesus? Second to that, did we act on what we saw? Was our life story (and is it now) riddled with the blindness that precipitates neglect?

Jesus' question in the Matthean message is a familiar one, for we have often asked it ourselves. Our own cries of dismay have begun: didn't you see...?

Didn't you see me crying? Didn't you notice my hunger, my thirst, my enslavement, my alienation, my isolation, my vulnerability? Didn't you see see that I was in pain and needed succor and solace? If you don't see my pain, how can you say you love me?

The core of the second challenge, however, goes beyond seeing. It lies in Christ's identification with all who suffer. He and they are one. Our blindness has critical and crucial consequences. If we lose sight of our brother or sister, we have lost sight of Christ himself! Blind to Christ, our shadow dance ends. Only death remains.

"For I was hungry and you gave me no food, I was thirsty and you gave me nothing to drink, I was a stranger and you did not welcome me, naked and you did not give me clothing, sick and in prison and you did not visit me" (Mt 25:42–43).

In our neglect—mine and yours—we fail to love the very Lord we profess to be our shepherd king. Inattentive to life, we have already chosen death. There lies our judgment.

There is comfort, however, even in the midst of the commanding challenge. There is mercy to temper justice. The consolation comes in the words of Ezekiel the prophet. Whether we are the perpetrators or the recipients of neglect, our solace is God's promise of rest and rescue. If no one else comes to save us, God is with us, shepherding rightly. "I myself will search for my sheep, and will seek them out....I will rescue them from all the places to which they have been scattered on a day of clouds and thick darkness....I myself will be the shepherd of my sheep, and I will make them lie down....I will seek the lost, and I will bring back the strayed, and I will bind up the injured, and I will strengthen the weak" (Ezek 34:11, 12, 15, 16).

This is today's hope and tomorrow's promise. It is the basis of our faith and trust. Challenged to be the best that we can be, urged to keep our eyes and hearts open, we are also eased by the warmth of God's shepherding love. Believing, we pray with Francis de Sales,

Have no fear for what tomorrow may bring. The same loving God who cares for you today will take care of you tomorrow and every day. God will either shield you from suffering or give you unfailing strength to bear it. Be at peace, then, and put aside all anxious thoughts and imaginations.

Know that our God reigns—and dances with us in the shadow of death!

For Reflection and Discussion

- Think about ways in which you can achieve balance in your life. Give examples that demonstrate your ability to dance with God in the shadow of death. How do you understand the statement: "Christ lives his life in you"?

Prayer

Dear God, I have no fear for what tomorrow may bring. I believe that you care for me today and will take care of me tomorrow and every day. I trust that you will either shield me from suffering or give me unfailing strength to bear it. I am at peace and have put aside all anxious thoughts and imaginations.

—Paraphrase of St. Francis de Sales prayer